Astonishing

Astonishing

Finding yourself, your purpose,
and your peace through a
more accurate view of Jesus

JUSTIN KENDRICK

Vox Publishing

ASTONISHING

Vox Publishing LLC
61 Amity Road
New Haven, CT 06515

Library of Congress Control Number: 2018914658
ISBN 978-1-7329594-0-8
eISBN 978-1-7329594-1-5

2019

Contents

Introduction

Since the day I met Jesus, I've been writing this book. Initially I didn't use pen and paper or type on the keyboard of a computer. This book began in the corners of my heart, then dominated the questions walking through my mind. Finally, it ended up in journal entries scribbled in notebooks over the last 20 years.

As a teenage kid, I would wake up before the sun every morning, open the Bible, and write down my thoughts and questions.

Why did Jesus have to die?
What was the meaning of his resurrection?
What's the point of the Old Testament stories?
How does it all fit together?

At my house today, I've got a large wooden chest filled with old notebooks. Half of what's in them doesn't even make sense to me now, but I can't bring myself to throw them out. They represent to me something sacred, something I find difficult to put into words.

In every notebook, there's a piece of my story. They are filled with thoughts and feelings that outline my progressive understanding of what Jesus actually accomplished when he came to Earth, died on the cross, and rose again.

I know I still have a long way to go. But I've come to believe that this truth of the gospel is the most important identity-defining, life-altering truth in the universe. It can't be known simply through the accumulation of information. These truths must be personally encountered. They must speak to you, shout at you, and eventually rewrite the script of your heart. Only the Spirit of Jesus can do that, but I've found that he's more than willing.

The prophet Jeremiah records the thoughts of God when he writes, "You will seek me and find me, when you seek me with all your heart." (Jer. 29:13) In other words, there is a formula to finding God. He can be found every time the formula is followed. Seek with all your heart. Make your pursuit of him more important than food or sleep or success, more important than anything. Seek him, and if you do, God will be found by you.

I wrote this book with the hope that if you haven't already, you would go buy yourself a notebook after you read what I've written. Consider this a small appetizer to the main course of the greatest study of your life. The more your heart understands what Jesus did, the more you will understand God, understand yourself, and understand the world around you.

My prayer is that this book makes you hungry. I pray that a new light is turned on, a new joy is realized, and a new hope settles down in the bedrock of your heart. I pray that this challenges your assumptions and awakens your appetite to fully discover the person and work of Jesus.

In the Gospel of Luke, Chapter Five, the author records one of the many miracles performed by Jesus. In this instance, a paralyzed man is lowered down through a roof right in front of where Jesus is teaching. Jesus forgives his sins, then heals his body. The response of those who witnessed the miracle is noteworthy.

"And amazement seized them all, and they glorified God and were filled with awe, saying, 'We have seen extraordinary things today.'" (Luke 5:26)

When was the last time you were seized with amazement? When was the last time you felt like that about God? Open your heart and ask him to do a profound work on the inside. He won't let you down.

1

The Beauty

You joyfully accepted the plundering of your property, since you knew that you yourselves had a better possession and an abiding one.
—Hebrews 10:34

I can't dance. I'd like to think that I can, and there have been moments in my life when I've convinced myself that I'm actually pretty good. But they don't last long. The reality is, I just don't have it. Most of us "can't dancers" end up congregating on the sidelines once the dancing gets going.

Maybe you've been there. You find yourself at a party or a wedding, and you may join in with the crowd for a few minutes. But you know your limits, and if the floor clears and eyes are on you, it's slow dance or no dance.

I was at a wedding recently hanging in the corner with a few other "can't dancers" when one particular woman took to the dance floor. She started moving her hips and swinging her arms like she just got hired for a 1980s Janet Jackson video. It wasn't pretty. It wasn't seductive.

It was … well … awkward.

At first, I assumed that she was not aware of her obvious lack of skill. We all have blind spots in our self-awareness. But the longer she danced, the more intrigued I became. A smile broke out over her face, and her movements grew more exaggerated. Soon, almost the entire wedding party had stopped dancing, but this one woman kept on going, unhindered by the dozens of eyes that were now locked on her. Didn't she know how ridiculous she looked? Didn't she know she couldn't really dance?

I was doing my best to hold back my laughter. There is something deeply comical about an awkward dancer. She was out there flopping around, and I was trying not to relish the pleasure of watching someone else look like a drowning sailor. Then my emotions changed, and I started feeling a little bad for her. She was making quite a spectacle of herself. But pity faded as I watched the expression on her face. Her countenance portrayed something unexpected. I realized that she *knew* she couldn't dance.

She just didn't care.

What started as comedy and converted to pity had now become a strange jealousy. There I was, sipping on my third soda, standing in the corner, self-conscious and safe. And there she was, in the center of the room, happy and confident and free. It was as if her flailing arms and unhindered smile proved to everyone in the room that she knew something inside that was bigger than the staring eyes or the critical thoughts. Somehow, she was so secure that she didn't bother with the approval of the people around her. Somehow, *her internal reality had transcended the external circumstance.* And that was stunning. It even made her dancing... well... beautiful.

I was amazed by what happened next. Pretty soon, other people began dancing around her, and within a few minutes, nearly every awkward "can't dancer" was on the floor spinning and smiling and sweating. She had unlocked the room, and it ended up being one of the loudest, most celebratory weddings I've ever attended.

But I still didn't dance. I wanted to and almost did, but in the end, I stood in the corner pretending I had something significant to do on my phone. That was as wild as my night got. I still think about that moment though, and I can see her right now spinning around smiling. For me, that night on the dance floor is an allegory of life. It's a picture of the person I want to be on the inside.

Because we all want to dance. We want to be unhindered. We want to live fully and freely. Most of us are spending our lives in a relentless pursuit of happiness, and we set our hopes on the improvement of our circumstances, expecting that to satisfy our hearts. Tragically, however, you can improve your job, your home, and your bank account, but these things don't guarantee an improvement in your soul. What we really need isn't happiness. What we really need is *joy*. And that's exactly what I hope to uncover in this book.

Joy is an internal reality that transcends external circumstances. It's the unique characteristic that marked the lives of the early Christians in the New Testament. In fact, once you start noticing the pattern, you see it everywhere amongst Jesus's earliest followers. In the Book of Acts, for example, we find Paul and Silas singing in jail. Singing? In jail?

Earlier that day, they were arrested for preaching about Jesus, beaten senseless, and thrown in prison in Philippi. At about midnight, when most people would be crying or complaining, these two men started singing. Their songs of praise were so powerful, the prison doors that held them swung open. (Acts 16:25–26)

In the Book of Hebrews, we're told of how the early followers of Jesus were persecuted for their faith. When Roman soldiers came and stole their possessions and burned their houses down, they "joyfully accepted" the results. (Heb. 10:34) Who does that?

Who sings after being unjustly beaten and thrown in prison? Have you ever met anyone who would smile and laugh as their home was ransacked and burned to the ground? Clearly these people knew something that most of us don't know. Their faith wasn't sterile and safe. It was alive and electric—even explosive. They could soar above the circumstances. They had real joy.

3

I remember years ago reading the story of Richard Wurmbrand, the Romanian pastor who spent over a decade of his life in prison, being tortured and enslaved for his faith in Christ. He talked about how, in the midst of suffering and loneliness, he discovered a well of joy that far exceeded any of life's comforts. He often found himself laughing and smiling even as he was interrogated, and his torturers were baffled by his behavior.[1]

Is that really possible? Could we discover a joy like that? And what would life look like if we did? What did Paul and Silas have that we lack? What did Richard Wurmbrand have that so radically altered his point of view? The answer is more obvious than we may think. *The truth that lived inside of them was so great that it pulled their hearts above the circumstances.*

Above the circumstances—that's an amazing idea. The problem is that most of us have never internalized a truth that powerful—and if we're honest, we're not even convinced that something like that exists. The world we live in is a global neighborhood, with information at our fingertips, and it leaves most of us feeling like we've seen it all. It takes a lot to surprise us or amaze us these days. We aren't easily impressed. But amidst all of the external stimuli, there remains an internal ache for something more. Your heart is thirsty for *joy*, and circumstantial happiness just can't satisfy the craving.

It may sound crazy, but I am convinced that there is a life of joy waiting for you. I believe that because I've sat at the table. I've tasted the wonder and the splendor, and the ache in my soul was both satisfied and intensified. If you want to experience real joy, you can't find it in your career or your relationships. You can't find it in your future plans or your family. As wonderful as these things are, they won't answer the cry of your heart. If you want to find joy, you have to find it in a story.

Not just any story, but one story in particular. That story is what the Scriptures call *the gospel*. The gospel in plain words means "good news."

It is what Christ accomplished for those who trust him. The gospel is what Paul and Silas were singing about in that jail cell. The gospel is what made those early Christians laugh and smile as they lost their homes. The gospel is the only truth that is actually *that* powerful.

This book was written in the hope that the beauty of the gospel could jump off these pages into your heart and do within you what only the gospel can do. Charles Spurgeon, a great preacher of another generation, said it like this:

> The gospel is the sum of wisdom, an epitome of knowledge, a treasure-house of truth; and a revelation of mysterious secrets. …Our meditation upon it enlarges the mind. And as it opens to our soul in successive flashes of glory, we stand astonished at the profound wisdom manifest in it. Ah, dear friends, if ye seek wisdom, ye shall see it displayed in all its greatness. …Here is essential wisdom: enthroned, crowned, glorified.[2]

Astonished. Can you remember the last time you felt that? Do you know what it means to be astonished? Maybe you felt it as a kid when you went outside on a clear night and tried to count the stars. Or the time you stood on the edge of the Grand Canyon and were overwhelmed by its beauty. Or maybe you felt it that day when you met the love of your life, or the first time you held your newborn child. But have you ever been astonished by the story of the gospel?

Spurgeon says that the gospel is essential wisdom—crowned and glorified. Our meditation on it "enlarges the mind." Those are big claims. How can the gospel be that good?

A More Manageable Size

If we're honest, for most of us the word "gospel" doesn't conjure up feelings of wonder and awe. It makes us think of something we already know, and already feel like we have a handle on. We think, *Yes, Christians believe Jesus died for our sins and rose again. That's great… but what about real life? What about my problems? What difference does that story really make for me?*

The gospel for many of us feels old. It feels known—like the movies we watched dozens of times as kids. We *know* the gospel. But somehow we've bleached the story of its wonder, and our surface understanding shields us from seeing its beauty. Frederick Buechner wrote of the danger of a bleached gospel.

> The preacher is apt to preach the Gospel with the high magic taken out, the deep mystery reduced to a manageable size. … The wild and joyful promise of the Gospel is reduced to promises more easily kept. The peace that passeth all understanding is reduced to peace that anybody can understand. The faith that can move mountains and raise the dead becomes faith that can help make life more bearable until death ends it.[3]

The gospel, reduced to a more manageable size. This is what we know so well. Maybe this is why the requirements of a holy life seem so limiting and unrealistic for many Christians. Why would we give up the pleasure of the moment if there is nothing more compelling to pursue? What would drive someone to forsake all and run from the pleasures of sin? Only a gospel so beautiful that it makes sin's imitation look ridiculous.

It was Tyrone Guthrie, the great theatrical director, who once said, "We are looking for ideas large enough to be afraid of again." How true. We're all looking—whether we realize it or not. We are looking because we have a deep inner need for a story that ties the stories of our lives together. We need a truth that rings higher and stands taller than our own opinions. We need a love that is more stable and consistent than our fragile attempts. The whole world is aching and longing for something so beautiful that it scares us, and inspires us, and calls us toward it.

The natural options all around us are not enough, and our world is getting tired of half answers. Sexual pleasure, faithful friendship, a perfect meal, inspiring entertainment, a sunset by the ocean—they all whisper to us. But not as *the* voice. They're only a reflection of the voice or an echo of it. They don't have the power to answer the deepest call of our hearts. The great questions still linger unsatisfied.

Who am I?
Who is God?
What is he like, and how does *he* view *me*?
Why am I here?
And why is my life significant?

Tragically, followers of Jesus rarely have compelling answers to these questions. If we are honest, most Christians aren't *that* joyful. We're annoyed when we get stuck in traffic, complain about the current political issues, and constantly mention the unresolved problems in our lives. Most Christians are "can't dancers," standing on the sidelines.

When I think of Paul and Silas singing in prison at midnight, or early believers joyfully accepting the plundering of their property, the chasm between us and them becomes all too obvious. The world is begging for something astonishing, and that something is hidden in the cross. It's up to us to seek it and find it and live the gospel without reducing the deep mystery to a more manageable size. We have to see it, taste it, internalize it, and feed off the joy it supplies. When we do that, the gospel becomes absolutely irresistible.

I love *The Message* translation of Ephesians 1:11. It simply states, "It's in Christ that we find out who we are and what we are living for."

That's it. One man, one story, has the power to reveal so much. But in order to be deeply changed, we must deeply drink. We must explore the covenant, understand the atonement, embrace justification, celebrate adoption, and apply resurrection. Hidden in the gospel there really is enough joy to make all of life shimmer and glow. But the depths must be explored.

In my own journey with God, it was the wonder of the gospel that provided my first taste of real joy. It was like electricity in my heart. The truth made its way into my soul and began shaking everything in me. I remember thinking, "Could this be true? Could this be real? Could this be everything I've been hoping for all along?" I've got a long way to go in my journey, but I haven't been disappointed yet.

In his letter to the Romans, the apostle Paul tells us that "faith comes from hearing, and hearing through the word of Christ." (Rom. 10:17) That Scripture is why I wrote this book. I believe that right now, God is awakening his people to the majesty of the gospel. It's when we hear the word *about Christ*—what he accomplished, what he has made available, and how he has changed everything—that faith starts to multiply, grows taller and taller, and reveals the glory of God.

I think back on the woman dancing her heart out at the wedding that night, and there's something I didn't notice at first glance: the real reason she was able to let herself go. I understand now the secret of her confidence. She could dance so freely and not concern herself with the opinions of the crowd because by her side, with his face reflecting an approving gaze, was the man she loved.

Her eyes were locked on her husband, and it didn't matter how she looked to the watching crowd, because it wasn't their approval she was looking for. It only mattered how she looked to him. And she knew from his smile that *he* loved her.

The bride is complete when she lives in the approving gaze of the bridegroom. This is the secret of joy. This is the gospel. Could it be that the gospel really is essential wisdom enthroned, crowned, and glorified? Could it be that our meditation on it actually does enlarge our minds? Could it be that Jesus is the husband of our hearts, and it's in him that we find the real secret to fully living?

There is a life full of promises kept, unwavering approval, and limitless love. There is a life of peace that actually *surpasses* understanding. Joy is not a fairy-tale myth; it can be found, and experienced, and it can grow. I want to invite you to join me on a great adventure. Let's explore together. Let's saturate our minds in what God has promised through the gospel, and discover what happens inside our hearts when we do this. I am sure of one thing: when you see it and taste it and remain in it, you can't help but be astonished.

DISCUSSION QUESTIONS

After reading the chapter, take time to reflect on the following questions. Then gather together with your small group and discuss your thoughts.

1. In your family when you were growing up, what did the "pursuit of happiness" look like? What did your family value or celebrate as success? How has your view of happiness or success changed over the years? What difference has Christ made in your thinking on this topic?

2. How can you relate to the person standing on the edge of the dance floor, unwilling to dance? Outline areas in your life where you have been hesitant to jump in. In your experience, what truths about God have been more difficult for you to embrace?

3. In this chapter, joy is described as "an internal reality that transcends external circumstances." Can you think of a time when you experienced this type of joy? What do you think hinders you from freely living in joy?

4. When truly internalized, the gospel is a source of astonishment, awe, and wonder. When was the last time you sensed this gospel-awe? What happened that inspired this awe?

5. Do you find yourself following a more reduced, manageable gospel? Why do you think that is so? In what ways has the good news of Christ become routine or normal to you? Why do you think this is the case? What can you do to reawaken your heart to the reality of what Jesus has done for you?

2

Covenant

We have this hope as an anchor for the soul, firm and secure. It enters the inner sanctuary behind the curtain, where our forerunner, Jesus, has entered on our behalf.

—Hebrews 6:19–20 NIV

M y brain only seems to work in English. I've tried to learn other languages. Five years of high school French, then four semesters of Spanish in college. I can vividly remember landing in Paris, hoping that the hours of study would pay off in real life. Nope. Nothing. I couldn't order a burger at a restaurant. My wife, however, has a section of her brain that seems to suck up languages like a sponge. After a week in Germany, she can carry a conversation with the locals.

Even though it doesn't come easily, language has always fascinated me. It seems to wrap itself around our personalities. If you think of any people group or culture, they just don't seem to be "them" if you take away their language. What's a German without his robust tone? Who are the Egyptians without their elegant, powerful Arabic?

Learning a foreign language isn't just a study in verbs and nouns, because every language is packed with nuance and culture. Imagine, for example, trying to learn English and hearing people use the word "run." One man says, "I have to run to the store." Did he really run there?

Another man says, "Run the numbers on that house." What does he mean by that? A third man says, "I have the runs!" and means something completely different than the first two!

Our personalities and our culture are tethered to our language, and learning a new language is in some ways like learning a whole new way of thinking. Language is more than communication; it's relationship. I can't imagine trying to get to know someone deeply without being able to speak the same language.

I remember when a friend first handed me the book *The Knowledge of the Holy* by A. W. Tozer. I picked it up and read the first statement: "What comes into our minds when we think about God is the most important thing about us."[1] Something about that hit me like a train. What do I think of first when my thoughts turn toward God? What informs my mental picture? Could it be that I've built an idea of God that is inconsistent with who he truly is? Could it be that I've never intentionally sought to learn *his* language?

From Genesis to Revelation, the Bible portrays a personal God who can be known. If that's true, and if really knowing God is possible, then what language does God speak?

Don't misunderstand. God doesn't just speak French or Italian or English. Language, at its core, is a vehicle, a method to transfer ideas or facts from one person to another. Let me show you through a simple illustration.

Learning Latin

My younger brother came home from high school freshman year and told me that he was choosing to study Latin for his foreign language. Latin? They still teach that? Isn't Latin, well...old? Forgotten? Outdated? Does anyone speak Latin anymore?

He proceeded to inform me that 60% of English words come from Latin. Over 40 languages are connected to it, and kids who learn it score statistically higher on their SATs.[2] Latin is one old, forgotten language that unlocks dozens of other languages. It forms a grid for thinking and processing facts that enables the learner to excel in science, math, and other languages. Latin is like a skeleton key; it opens a lot more than one door.

The language of God is like Latin. It's rarely spoken in our day. It's old and often forgotten, but once you learn it, his language unlocks the greatest and most important doors in life. If we want to have a clear picture of God, then our only option is to submerge ourselves in his native language so that in the end we can clearly know his heart. Though he can communicate in various ways, God has a primary tongue.

God speaks the language *of promise.*

Promise? That's a language? You sure he doesn't speak Hebrew? Greek? Aramaic? Of course, God isn't limited to a human language, and when he wants to communicate with humanity, he uses the primary vehicle of *promises* to transfer the message. The Scriptures are a collection of the promises he has made. Someone once counted nearly 7,500 promises from Genesis to Revelation.[3] Like Latin, *promises* form a grid that enables us to see him and to see life as he intended it. Once the grid is built, every aspect of life becomes clearer.

Unfortunately, promises in our day are not as popular as they once were. There was a time when two people would shake hands and give their lives to keep the promise they made, but that day is long gone. Today, promises must be signed, stamped, witnessed, and upheld in court—and even then they're often not taken seriously. For many of us, even the word "promise" leaves a bad taste in our mouths.

Your dad promised to stick around after the divorce, but that didn't happen.

Your first boyfriend promised to love you forever, but that lasted four weeks.

Your roommate in college promised not to use your toothpaste. Then it disappeared.

Life is full of failed promises.

At this point in our world, we almost expect them to fail. It drives me nuts how often in movies the characters promise things they can't control. They say things like, "Stay here, I promise I'll be back to get you," as they head off for war. Then they get shot in the first battle. They promise, "I'll love you forever," and the next scene they have moved on to someone else.

Promises don't seem to mean much in our culture anymore, but there's another reason we often have an aversion to promises. Maybe you've made a few promises to God and didn't keep them yourself. You went to the front of the church after a service, prayed a heartfelt prayer, and then went out the next weekend and did exactly what you promised God you'd never do again. It happens once. Then twice. Soon even your own promises seem to lose their substance and become empty.

The problem is that if you haven't deeply internalized God's language of promise, close relationship with him just isn't possible. You can sing the songs, pray the prayers, and hope for the best, but listening to someone speak a language you don't understand is only interesting for a few minutes. Pretty soon it just sounds like noise. Religion. Repetition. Routine. Many Christians I know feel like God is speaking in Swahili. They want to know God. They want to hear God. But if they're honest, they feel disconnected.

Maybe you feel disconnected from God because your heart has never taken ahold of his promises. Yet Scripture says, "Draw near to God, and he will draw near to you." (James 4:8) In other words, if you will devote yourself to learning God's language and practicing God's language, he will come closer to you. You will encounter his presence and establish real relationship with the Creator of life, and you will find a storehouse of joy that has no borders and a fountain of love far beyond measure. I promise you, this is worth your attention.

Let's Take a Road Trip

I want to invite you on a brief journey through the Old Testament to help build an understanding of God's language. Throughout the Bible, promises are often introduced by a different name. God frequently makes a sacred agreement between himself and his people, and these agreements are called *covenants*. A covenant is an oath-bound relationship. The covenants found in Scripture form what's been described as "the backbone" of the Bible. All of God's interaction with us is supported by this backbone.

The first covenant we see in Scripture is formed between God and our first parents, Adam and Eve. The way God creates the Earth helps us understand the type of relationship he intended for humanity. When he creates vegetation for example, he doesn't just say, "Let there be trees." Instead, he speaks to the earth and says, "Let the earth sprout vegetation." (Gen. 1:11) He creates fish not by saying, "Let there be fish," but by speaking to the sea.

Why would God do this? He is trying to show us an important pattern. God speaks to the natural environment created to sustain the creature and commands it to bring forth the creature. So trees can't survive without being rooted in the earth. Fish can't breathe if they're taken out of the water.

When God creates people, however, he doesn't speak to the earth or the sea, because the essence of humanity is not earthly. Instead, he speaks to himself. He says, "Let us make man in our image." (1:26) Father, Son, and Holy Spirit. One God in three persons, creating humanity in the image of God with an eternal soul. Like water to a fish, or earth to a tree, God created people to only live *through* him. He is the oxygen of the human soul. To remove God from man is to pull the tree from the earth. The life source has been severed, and soon the tree stops breathing. God's original design for humanity was that he was the oxygen that kept us fully alive. This is where our understanding of God begins.

In his covenant with our first parents, God gives them dominion on the Earth, resources, and an unbroken relationship to himself.
Adam's responsibility was to use what God gave him and honor God
as his source. But you know the story. Our first parents entertain what
some theologians have called "the Great Lie." *God can't be fully trusted.*
So they question his intentions. They wonder if he is somehow limiting
their potential. They choose to eat from the forbidden tree in pursuit
of being equals with God. They want autonomy. They don't want to be
dependent on him like the fish is on the sea. This resistance to God-
dependence breaks the covenant agreement between Adam and God.

Here is where we must pause and learn something about God's language of promise. To God, Adam was not just one man. He was *the* man.
He represented our entire race. And when he chose independence from
God, it didn't just change his fate—it changed his DNA. The corrupting
agent called sin entered the genetic code of humanity. It seeped into the
bones of our first father, and he has since passed it on to every one of his
children.

This is what the apostle Paul meant when he wrote, "When Adam
sinned, sin entered the world. Adam's sin brought death, so death spread to
everyone, for everyone sinned." (Rom. 5:12 NLT) As our representative,
Adam corrupted his seed with his sin, and God made everything to produce
its own kind. The seed he passed on to his children was infected with the
disease.

(As you read this right now, it may sound more and more like a foreign language. Stick with it. Every foreign language feels unnatural at
first.)

God saw Adam as the representative of humanity, and Adam's sin
brought sin into our DNA. What was the result? Brokenness.

First, there was a deep internal brokenness. Adam and Eve *felt* naked.
(Gen. 3:7) In other words, they felt exposed, vulnerable, incomplete.
They felt an internal compulsion to hide or cover up their true selves.

Have you ever felt that way? I know I have. Maybe you feel like you're not smart enough or pretty enough. Maybe you feel dirty because of some past failure. Maybe you feel empty and nothing seems to fill the void. Not the relationships, not the kids, not the dog. Maybe you feel stuck. These are all symptoms of the deeper disease. We feel empty or lonely or anxious or fearful or unwanted, all because of sin.

There is something broken deep down inside all of us. Something we can't control or cover up, as if the very core of our hearts are warped or out of joint. Within one generation of Adam's sin, Cain was bashing his brother's head in with a rock, and this was just the beginning of the brokenness.

Have you recognized in your own heart this deep sense of brokenness? It's those compulsive thoughts about that other woman, even though you love your wife. It's that secret addiction that haunts you that you haven't told anyone about. It's those irrational fears that paralyze you when you're on an airplane or sitting at home alone. Maybe you're spending way too much time on WebMD because you're scared of a disease you don't even have. Maybe you're spending way too much time on social media because everyone else's life looks perfect and yours feels empty. Jealousy, anger, unforgiveness, lust, fear.

These are all results of the brokenness that sin has caused in our hearts. But the damage goes much deeper than that. In fact, the whole world has slipped out of joint. God said to Adam, "Cursed is the ground because of you…thorns and thistles it shall bring forth for you." (Gen. 3:17–18) Humanity's sin brought forth thorns. The Earth itself is hemorrhaging under the weight of sin and everyone suffers from this brokenness.

After sin entered the human heart, God forced Adam out of the garden. The place of friendship and nearness to God was no longer accessible. It wasn't accessible to him, his children, or his children's children. Mankind broke the covenant, and there is nothing we can do to repair the relationship. God is just, and he will not ignore or compromise his justice. But sin did not take God by surprise. In fact, he always had a plan to reveal himself through our brokenness and turn pain into glory.

Pay Attention to Shadows

Once Adam broke the covenant with God, the Scripture records a host of other covenants made between God and people. God made a covenant with Noah, and then later with Abraham and Sarah. He made a covenant with Moses and the nation of Israel, and then again with David.

Finally, God reveals that all of these covenant promises are shadows or symbols of a greater and more perfect covenant. Just like a shadow resembles the person it belongs to, each covenant promise resembles the final covenant that will reverse the work of sin in our hearts. A shadow doesn't have all the details. You can't tell a person's hair color or skin color by their shadow, but you can see their basic shape. With each of these Old Testament covenants, God was revealing to us the basic shape of his future covenant. Remember, he is teaching humanity his language, and he speaks the language of promise. God knows that nothing teaches truth better than a story, so he did something brilliantly unexpected.

God uses the real stories of human history to outline his rescue plan for humanity.

With every character in the story, God reveals more and more about his plan to save us. But each time, the revelation seems counterintuitive. It goes against our natural assumptions and catches us off guard. God's plan for restoration is foreshadowed in the covenant promises of the Old Testament, so that when the perfect covenant appeared, it could be recognized and embraced by those who have eyes to see it. Let's look at a few examples together.

In the covenant God makes with Noah, for example, we often assume that he chose Noah because he was a good guy and everyone else was evil. That's the natural train of thought. God blesses the good guys and punishes the bad guys, so we should try to be good. But that's not what the story actually says. It tells us first that before he had done good or bad, "Noah found *favor* in the eyes of the Lord." (6:8) Favor? Yes. Favor, by definition, is unearned and undeserved. In other words, God chose Noah and favored him, not because Noah was good, but because God was good. The text later tells us that Noah was righteous and blameless, and that he walked with God.

Did Noah's good deeds lead to him being favored? The Scripture actually implies that it was the other way around. Noah was favored (undeservedly loved and accepted), and that favor led to his righteousness. So he wasn't loved because he obeyed. Rather, Noah believed that he was given love freely, and obedience flowed from a heart that had encountered undeserved love. This distinction makes all the difference in the world!

Then we're told that Noah climbs into an ark to save himself and his family from the flood. The story gives us an exhaustive amount of detail when it comes to the dimensions of the ark. It tells us the exact width and height. Why? Does the writer think we really care how many cubits long this boat is? Is he giving us the specifics assuming we'll want to build one later at home? Why include so many details about the size of the ark?

Unless the boat itself isn't *just* a boat. It's a picture. It's one of God's "shadows" to reveal his future covenant promise. Remember, God is painting a picture of his plan of restoration through the story. That's why the dimensions of the boat aren't actually recorded to describe the boat. They are recorded to describe *the man.*

A man?

Interestingly enough, the dimensions of the ark described in the story are the exact proportions of a man lying down. Saint Augustine, one of the great church fathers, said it this way:

For even its very dimensions, in length, breadth, and height, represent the human body... For the length of the human body, from the crown of the head to the sole of the foot, is six times its breadth from side to side, and ten times its depth or thickness, measuring from back to front: that is to say the measure of a man as he lies on his back or on his face, he is six times as long from head to foot as he is broad from side to side, and ten times as long as he is high from the ground. And therefore the ark was made 300 cubits in length, 50 in breadth, and 30 in height.[4]

So the story of Noah and the ark, and the covenant that follows, isn't just a story about Noah. God is pointing to something else! He is describing *someone* else. He is pointing to a future covenant that will be initiated by his divine favor, just as it was with Noah. To receive this covenant, you must be like Noah and enter "into" the ark—a man. The story speaks of a man who will provide shelter for all those who will run to him. A man who is lying down! The ark, with a skylight pointing up and only one door on its side represents a man who kept his eyes pointed up and was pierced in his side. God's plan is that a dead man becomes the ark of life! Maybe this sounds foreign to you, or maybe some of God's language is beginning to make sense. The story of Noah is really about *Jesus*.

But that's just a taste. Later, God makes a covenant with Abraham that he will bless him and bless the world through him, but Abraham isn't convinced that God will follow through, and he has the guts to ask a question: *How will I know, God? How can I be sure of this?* (15:8) What follows is a strange response from the invisible God speaking the language of promise. He tells Abraham to slaughter a few animals and cut them in half. He then waits until Abraham falls asleep, and while he is sleeping, God appears. He appears as a fire and passes in between the slaughtered animals. He then says, "Know for certain Abraham...I will do this." (15:13)

What is happening here? Abraham knew exactly what had happened, and it gave him great assurance. In his culture, if two kings or two great leaders sought to make an unbreakable promise, they would go through this particular ritual. They would slaughter these certain animals, and the lesser king would first walk between them, promising to uphold his end of the covenant. He would say, "If I break my promise, kill me like you did these animals." Then the greater king would go through the same routine.

But in Abraham's case, God does something surprising. He has Abraham prepare the sacrifice, then lets him rest! God himself walks through on behalf of both parties, effectively saying, "If I break my promise to you, let it be done to me as it was done to these animals. But if you break your promise to me, let it also be *done to me* as it was done to these animals."

In other words, God promises to fulfill both sides of the covenant. But wait. God can't do that, can he? God can't be *killed* because *we* broke our promise to him...can he? How can he fulfill the role of both God and man—unless his plan is to become a man and live the life of obedience that Adam never did? What we see here is a shadow. Through the stories of the Old Testament, God is showing us the shadow of his future covenant.

The Purpose Behind the Shadow

God later makes a covenant with Moses and the people of Israel. As slaves in Egypt, they are told to take the blood of an unblemished male lamb and wipe it on the doorpost of their home. (Ex. 12:7) That night, God brings judgment on Egypt, but every Hebrew is spared. Why does judgment pass over them? Was it because they were good people? Was it because of their good deeds?

That's not the reason given in the story. Just as Noah found favor with God and it led to a life of obedience, and just as Abraham was blessed and God promised to uphold both sides of the agreement, the only reason the people of Israel were safe was because they stayed in the house marked with the blood. The good people, the bad people, the nice people, the mean people—if they were in the house marked by the blood, they were saved! The blood of the lamb made them righteous.

Later, when Israel is delivered from Egypt, God outlines his covenant promises to them. They are instructed to build a temple and appoint a high priest. Each year, an unblemished lamb is sacrificed for the sin of the people in the most sacred room in the temple, the Holy of Holies. But this practice is another one of God's shadows, planted in the story to point us to something else. There is one high priest, who will enter into heaven itself with the shed blood of a perfect sacrifice, and this sacrifice will wash away the sin of the world.

In fact, every story of the Old Testament serves more than one purpose. Every story is an arrow pointing to God's great conclusion. Why did Jonah spend three days in the deep? Why did Isaac need to be put on the altar? And what about Daniel and Esther and David? God, in his unfathomable wisdom, used human history to paint a great portrait of his better covenant.

But the stories all come together when you deeply understand the greatest story. Reading the Old Testament without understanding the cross is like reading only Chapters 1 and 7 in a 15-chapter mystery novel. Only the gospel allows the pieces to fit in the proper place.

Jesus is the ark that Noah ran into. He is a man lying down in death, the only one who can rescue us. And by his death, we can find life.

Jesus is the King who walked between Abraham's slaughtered animals. He represented both sides of the agreement, both God and man, and was punished because we broke our promise to God. Like the animals that Abraham slaughtered, he was torn in two by the people he created, so that God could bless us through him. And he did it while we were unaware of what he was doing, fast asleep and oblivious like Abraham!

Jesus is the lamb whose blood was smeared on the threshold of the house in Egypt. If we stay *in* him, no judgment befalls us. He rescues all who run to him and they are saved not because they are good, but because they stay inside the house.

Jesus is the High Priest who entered the Holy of Holies to make a sacrifice for the sin of the people. He did not enter a temple made by men. Rather, he entered heaven itself, with scars on his hands and scars on his feet. He was the priest and the lamb, and his sacrifice was more than enough.

Jesus is the second Adam. Just as the first Adam represented all people and passed on the seed of sin, Christ came as a second representative. He wasn't born from the seed of a man, but was born of a virgin by the Spirit and passes on the Holy Spirit to all who receive him. When Pontius Pilate brought Jesus before the raging crowd and declared, "Behold the man!" he hardly knew the significance of what he had said. Jesus was not a man. He was in fact *the man*. What happened to Jesus counts not just for himself but for all who come to him.

Do you think it was a coincidence that the Romans put a crown of thorns on his head? "And the soldiers twisted together a crown of thorns and put it on his head." (John 19:2) No. It wasn't. Those were Adam's thorns. Those were the symbol of the curse. He wore it as a crown so that the wrath of God and the curse of the Earth would be emptied on him, and the promise of God to bless us would stand.

The shadow of Jesus hangs over the entire Bible. Every Old Testament story points to a better covenant. God's perfect holiness required justice, but his love compelled him to mercy, so he built the covenant not on the instability of our good works, but on the only thing that cannot be shaken. He put on skin, lived the life we could not, and transferred the benefits to our account. He built the covenant on himself, on his own stability and faithfulness. This made the promise unshakable.

Words fail to express the wonder of God's covenant with us through Jesus. The writer of the Book of Hebrews, in an attempt to articulate the implications of the New Covenant, said it like this:

> We have this hope as an anchor for the soul, firm and secure. (Heb. 6:19 NIV)

An anchor for the soul. Just as a boat needs an anchor or it will drift out to sea, so your soul needs something that will never fail. Family will fail. Friends will fail. Your body will fail. Your mind will fail. In the end, time itself will fail you.

But the promise won't. *This* promise won't. We see its shadow in the thorns of Adam. We recognize its reflection in the ark of Noah. We smell its fragrance as Abraham gazes upon the stars and believes in a God who loves him. Every story whispers. Every word points beyond itself. Every shadow builds our assurance.

God has promised to come close to us. This is his native language. This is how he speaks. And he never breaks a promise.

> "But this is the new covenant I will make with the people of Israel after those days," says the Lord. "I will put my instructions deep within them, and I will write them on their hearts. I will be their God, and they will be my people. And they will not need to teach their neighbors, nor will they need to teach their relatives, saying, 'You should know the Lord.' For everyone, from the least to the greatest, will know me already," says the Lord. "And I will forgive their wickedness and I will never again remember their sins." (Jer. 31:33–34 NLT)

DISCUSSION QUESTIONS

1. What stood out to you most in this chapter? What stirred your heart or pricked your conscience? What did you sense God saying to you personally as you read?

2. A. W. Tozer said that "what comes into your mind when you think about God is the most important thing about you. It deeply shapes the way you see the world." In light of this, what comes naturally into your mind when you first think about God?

3. Think back over your life. What has your experience been with others keeping the promises they made to you? Can you think of a time when someone you trusted deeply let you down? How well do you feel you keep your promises to others? Can you think of a time when you let someone down?

4. The Great Lie whispers to us that God cannot be trusted. It causes us to question his intentions and believe that God wants to limit our potential. Think about all the realms of your life— home, friendships, finances, job, hopes, dreams...everything. What areas do you sense are infected with this lie? What truths from this chapter refute that lie? What steps can you take this week to embrace those truths?

5. God's promises are a firm and secure anchor for the soul. What promises do you sense the Holy Spirit speaking to you today for your marriage, friendships, health, finances, job, or another area of life? What promise from the Scripture can you hold on to this week?

3

Atonement

Fear not, little flock, for it is your Father's good pleasure to give you the kingdom.

—Luke 12:32

She steps into the middle of the stage. Clutching her guitar, she smiles timidly at the four judges sitting in front of her. The band around her begins to play, and she starts to sing, introducing her voice to the world. She's on "America's Got Talent," and this is her moment.

The crowd and the judges sit back in awe as the young woman sings her heart out. It's an amazing performance.

Later, in an interview she's asked, "What would it mean for you to win this competition?"

She pauses, pulls back, hesitates. "Everything," she replies. "It would mean everything."

I'm not sure if you've noticed, but the world has officially become obsessed with talent shows. Of course, they are nothing new. As far back as the human race can remember, people have gathered to display their unique abilities. But it seems today, around the world, these shows are getting more and more traction. The contestant comes forward, prepared to showcase their unique ability, and when asked what being on the show means to them, the response seems almost automatic.

"Everything. This means everything."

That sounds a bit overstated, don't you think? Does it really mean *everything*? In other words, four judges who don't know you, don't understand your life, and haven't spent three minutes with you are now going to determine your value in front of millions of viewers around the world? They are somehow uniquely qualified to decide your future and their approval means *everything* to you? If they celebrate you, then you are special, but if they reject you, then all your deepest fears are confirmed. Your future rides on this 90-second audition.

And we can't help but watch.

There's something intriguing and exciting about the whole thing. The contestant will either launch into fame and stardom or become the joke at the office the next day. As we sit on the edges of our couches, something about the whole process pricks our hearts. If you're anything like me, you've found yourself almost brought to tears as you've watched an insecure young kid earn the approval of Simon Cowell. It's a magical moment.

Somewhere deep down, we all identify with the person on the stage. We know a small taste of the pressure they're feeling, because that stage already exists in our own minds.

Psychologists tell us that the human psyche is hardwired for approval. From our earliest days on Earth, we each start building our own sense of identity, and we'll use whatever materials we can get our hands on. Take your success at a sport and add your good grades in math class. Then mix in the attention you got from those girls in middle school and the praise from your younger brother. Now you're starting to feel good. But there are some troubling parts to the equation too. Your dad always made you feel like you weren't good enough, and some kids in the neighborhood constantly made fun of your big ears. You're a slow reader, and the teacher had to put you in a "special class" so you could keep up. Before you know it, there are some cracks in the foundation.

Add an alcoholic parent, a few heartbreaks, and a couple bad decisions. These may just sound like random things, but your mind takes these moments and uses them to construct your identity. If the right button is pushed or the right brick is knocked out of place, the structure could begin to wobble or even collapse.

Most of us try to strengthen our sense of identity with a little game of comparison. Have you ever found yourself on social media and you come across an old friend from high school? Before you realize it, you're in the middle of a full-on investigation.

"Who did they marry? Oh, their kids are kind of funny looking. They've definitely put on some weight... Wow, that's an amazing house they bought... it's much nicer than mine."

I was recently speaking with a friend who was so excited to find out that the most handsome, popular kid in high school was now 50 pounds overweight and bald. My friend was walking around with this guy's photo, making sure everyone knew that he was no longer the best-looking person from school. My first response in this moment was self-righteousness.

I wouldn't gloat about another man's problems. I wouldn't show everyone an unflattering picture of someone else.

But the more I reflected on the moment, the more I realized that I do this all the time. I see within myself the subtle inclination to cheer when someone else fails. I see within myself the propensity to compete with people I don't even know. With a few minutes of honest reflection, you might see this tendency in yourself too. Why do we care? Why do we need others to fail in order to feel like we're succeeding?

Sometimes, after a few minutes on social media, we walk away from the screen feeling a little more important. A little more secure. Other times, we walk away feeling like we're a step behind. A step behind *whom* exactly?

If you're anything like me, you're a step behind the invisible person you've been racing all your life. Why do I compare myself to others to gain a sense of value? Why do I work into a conversation the fact that I know an important person or did a significant thing? Why am I so thirsty for a pat on the back or a moment of recognition? How did we all get so insecure?

There's a story in the Old Testament about Jacob's son Joseph and his God-inspired dream. Joseph shares his dreams of being a great ruler with his brothers, and they hate him for it. They view his high calling as an assault on their value. They assume that his promotion means their demotion. Joseph can't be a great ruler, because to them his success is an indictment on their worth. These older brothers are so insecure that they eventually conspire to kill Joseph. Where does insecurity like that come from? The Scripture gives us a clue in Genesis 37:4.

But when his brothers saw that their father loved him more than all his brothers, they hated him and could not speak peacefully to him.

Their insecurity was rooted in a desperate cry for their father's love. They felt overlooked by him. Their hearts were carrying the sting of his rejection, so they needed to compare themselves to others to solidify their own sense of worth. It seems crazy that these 10 brothers would be so insecure that their father's choice to play favorites would drive them to murder. Why did the approval of their dad mean so much? Why couldn't they just move on?

They couldn't move on for the same reason you and I can't. These 10 jealous brothers offer us a window into the hidden room of our own hearts. The truth is that *every insecurity is rooted in an uncertainty of the Father's love.* Unshakable identity can't be built on talent or accomplishment or family or ethnicity. At the core, only the Creator, the Eternal Father, can secure your identity. We have a tendency to project this need on our earthly dad, but no matter how perfect he may have been, the wound still exists. Our hearts yearn for divine approval. Our hearts ache to know that we are right with God. As Brennan Manning succinctly stated, "The deepest desire of our hearts is for union with God. God created us for union with himself. This is the original purpose of our lives."[1] And nothing short of an ironclad guarantee of his approval will ever satisfy.

And this is where the real problem comes into view. Deep down, in the dark places of your soul, you know that you have failed. You know that you carry sin, and the record of your life doesn't provide any sense of assurance that God accepts you. The subconscious disease that lives in your bones reminds you again and again. You are a sinner. You are unacceptable. Just look at what you've done. God sees it all. How could he ever accept you?

The holiness of God is written throughout the pages of Scripture. There is no mistaking that the God of the Bible is perfectly holy. There is no evil in him. There is no crookedness in him. His holiness is one of his most mysterious and terrifying characteristics, because if he is holy, then clearly I cannot be in union with him. My heart knows it. My soul knows it. There is a distance between me and God. "Without holiness, no one will see the Lord." (Heb. 12:14 NIV)

But sin does more than cause separation. Sin requires justice. Of all of God's attributes, his wrath is probably the least popular. In our politically correct world, we sometimes struggle to see how someone could be both good and full of wrath. We pretend like "being good" means letting hurtful behavior slide and never executing justice. But if God is to intensely love what is good, he must intensely hate what is evil.

Would a judge be good if he let criminals go free? Whose fault would it be if the criminal left the courtroom and committed the same crime the next day? Would a husband be good if he didn't try to stop someone from murdering his wife? Would a world leader be good if he allowed a foreign nation to invade? Being good requires being just, and justice demands that people are held accountable for their behavior.

Could we respect and trust a God who was not enraged when a little boy is beaten senselessly by his dad, or a little girl is raped by her uncle, or an irresponsible mom abandons her kids at a playground and never returns? God loves people, but he hates sin. He makes his perspective clear: "I am watching them closely, and I see every sin. They cannot hope to hide from me." (Jer. 16:17 NLT) Principled. Controlled. Fierce wrath. This is God.

In fact, we are told that God is keeping track of every sin ever committed. Each sin has a just penalty. The psalmist describes it like this: "For in the hand of the Lord, there is a cup [of His wrath], with foaming wine, well mixed; and He pours out from it, and all the wicked of the earth shall drain it down to the dregs." (Psalm 75:8)

God has a cup where he has calculated the wrath and just penalty for all sin, and the guilty must drink. Many of the Old Testament prophets pick up this theme a number of times. Ezekiel calls it the cup of horror. Jeremiah, the cup of wrath. Isaiah, the cup of staggering. God is keeping track. He can't be fooled and he can't just let it go.

The combination of these truths sends the human psyche into a tailspin. We ache and thirst for approval that only God himself can give, and yet we simultaneously know that we are sinful. Our hearts often scramble to justify ourselves or compare our sin with someone else's, but these excuses can't provide assurance. Written on the tablet of our conscience is the truth of the justice and wrath of God. Sin deserves judgment. Where can you turn? Where can you hide?

The Two Thieves

Thousands of years of history have shown that people generally run to one of two hiding places. The ancient church father Tertullian said it like this: "Just as Jesus was crucified between two thieves, so the gospel is ever crucified between these two errors."[2] Our hearts need somewhere to find approval and acceptance, and so we turn to either religion or relativism.

By religion, I mean specifically that tendency in all of us to try to earn our way to God. *Do your best to do what's right. Give money, help the less fortunate, attend church. Show kindness. Be a moral person.* Slowly, often unnoticeably, your good deeds become the source of your confidence. Eventually, the inner voice of rejection can be quieted by your flurry of good activity. *You really are a good person.*

But the voice of guilt and shame returns. So you do more, give more, proving to yourself again and again that you are good. But it isn't enough. The end result of religion is predetermined. You either live in a cycle of guilt and self-effort, or pride takes root and you convince yourself that you really are *good*. Either way, religion will never lead to a deep union with God, a deep experience of love, or a deep well of joy. It never fully answers your cry for acceptance. You're still stuck on the stage looking to your boss, or your boyfriend, or your dad, or your someone else, to answer the question that only God can answer.

So we turn to relativism. If religion is my attempt to conform to the rules, relativism is my attempt to rewrite them. Relativism says that if I can't earn my way to God, then I'll adjust my view of God to fit my condition.

God can't possibly be that holy. Doesn't he accept everyone just as they are? He's forgiving and kind and willing to look past my shortcomings. I like what the Bible says about love, but when it comes to sexuality, or money, those things are pretty outdated...

Relativism gives the individual permission to believe in a god that best suits them. The tragedy of relativism is that though you may succeed in convincing yourself that you're very "spiritual," a gnawing emptiness will linger close behind. The emptiness exists because the god you worship isn't God—it's *you*. You made God into your own image. Self-worship may satisfy for a season, but sooner or later, the ache of your soul will resurface. Just like the tree needs the earth and the fish needs the water, you need God. He is the oxygen of your soul, and creating your own version of God will never lead to real joy or fulfillment.

As you saw in the last chapter, the Old Testament reveals the shadow of Jesus. We can see his frame, but not his face. His shadow emerges again in the practice of animal sacrifice. But before we get into the details of animal sacrifice in the Bible, it's important to pause.

We live in a very sterilized world—the world of hand sanitizer and neatly packaged meat products. Animal sacrifice, or killing animals for anything, is foreign territory for most of us. We don't regularly interact with blood like earlier generations did. For them, killing animals was a regular part of the week. For us, animals and blood are often unknown realities. When was the last time, for example, you ripped the head off a chicken, pulled out its feathers, drained its carcass, and cooked it over a fire? It probably didn't happen in the last 48 hours. With that in mind, do your best to get past the squeamish feelings and downright "strangeness" of this reality. Try to see this physical act as a shadow of a spiritual act.

Under the Old Testament law, nearly everything needed to be made holy is through sacrifice. If you sinned intentionally, you made a sacrifice to pay for your sin. If you sinned unintentionally, you made a sacrifice again. If you touched something unclean, dishonored your neighbor, or broke any of God's commands in the law, a sacrifice was required.

The law required all types of sacrifices. A pigeon, a dove, a bull, a goat—various animal sacrifices for various sins. In the time in which we live, this type of ritual seems barbaric and uneducated, but God was trying to teach his people a critically important spiritual principle. Sin causes death, and if a holy God is to forgive sin, then life must be traded for the death caused by sin. Life is found in its purest form in only one place.

For the life of the body is in its blood. I have given you the blood on the altar to purify you, making you right with the Lord. It is the blood, given in exchange for a life, that makes purification possible. (Lev. 17:11 NLT)

God put life in blood. Any medical doctor will tell you that. But it's not just physical life. The physical and the spiritual overlap, and blood has spiritual significance. "Without the shedding of blood, there is no forgiveness of sins." (Heb. 9:22) The Old Testament chronicles the story of how people twist the law of God either into religion or relativism. At one point, they're obedient and proud, confident in their own ability to please God. This is religion. In the next generation, they ignore his commands and try to create their own way to God. This is relativism.

All along, the law was not introduced to bring people into perfect union with God, but to expose our sin and reveal our need for a savior. The law shows us that we cannot be the source of salvation. We cannot be good enough or holy enough. We cannot create our own way to God. It reveals the truth that we have desperately sought to avoid:

I am helpless. And I cannot fix myself.

Like the stories of Noah and Abraham and David and Esther, the sacrificial requirements of the law were an arrow pointing to God's perfect plan of redemption, because God put life in the blood.

If life is in the blood, and God is perfectly just, then death and judgment must come to all to pay for the debt of sin. What else could wash away the sin of the world? With so much sin in this broken world, what other sacrifice would be so valuable that it could pay for sin and satisfy the justice of God?

It would seem that humanity is hopeless. There is no blood that powerful. There is no life that precious. The only one with that much life is God himself. But God is spirit, not flesh and blood. How could he ever wash away our sins?

Back to the Garden

The passion of Jesus is a term used to recount the final days before his death. This phrase typically describes the events that begin with his entrance into Jerusalem. He is then seen around the table with his disciples. Before he is betrayed, Jesus finds his way into a garden to spend the night in prayer.

> And they went to a place called Gethsemane. And he said to his disciples, "Sit here while I pray." (Mark 14:32)

It's significant that of all the places he could have chosen, he picks a garden. It was in the garden that Adam and Eve first doubted God's intentions, and their disobedience led to the fracture between God and humanity. Now it's in the garden called Gethsemane that God will inaugurate his plan to reestablish relationship. Jesus knew exactly what he was doing.

The word *Gethsemane* means oil press. It was a place where olive trees flourished, and workers would beat the trees, allowing all the ripe olives to fall off. They would then crush the olives using a millstone, and a reddish substance similar to blood would ooze out. This oil would be collected and used for lamps, among other things. Jesus was coming to the garden because he knew that he would be beaten and then crushed until his blood was poured out. He also knew that the blood he shed would be collected and used for the great lamp that would light the world. He invited his disciples to pray with him, when something unexpected happened.

> And He took with Him Peter and James and John, and began to be struck with terror and amazement and deeply troubled and depressed. (Mark 14:33 AMPC)

Jesus became struck with terror? Consider that for a moment. Jesus is the one who walked on water, calmed the storm, rose Lazarus from the dead, stood up to the Pharisees. Jesus was always in control. He never caved to pressure. He never expressed any worry or doubt about *anything*. He wasn't terrified when the boat was sinking, or the demonic man was screaming, or the child was dying. Yet here, for the first time in the Gospels, we find Jesus struck with terror. What could possibly terrify him? Was he afraid to die? No. Men of much lesser courage had bravely faced death. Was he afraid of the Roman guards? No. He had stood up to them many times before. It wasn't death or pain or the Romans or the Pharisees that caused Jesus to stagger in terror in the garden. It was what Jesus saw in the garden that overwhelmed his heart.

> And he said, "Abba, Father, all things are possible for you. Remove this cup from me." (Mark 14:36)

This cup? *What* cup? In the Garden of Gethsemane, God the Father allowed God the Son to see the cup of wrath that he must drink if he was to wash away the sin of the world. It was the cup that the psalmist said overflowed with the judgment of God. It was the cup of terror. The cup of horror. In this cup was all the wrath of God for all the sin of man. This is what Jesus saw in the garden. And he staggered.

God's plan of redemption was not for you to earn your way to holiness. His plan was not for you to create your own path back to God. His plan, foreshadowed in the Old Testament and revealed in Jesus, was to drink the judgment for sin himself. In the garden, Jesus fully embraced his mission, and the pressure caused his blood vessels to rupture and his body to sweat blood. He was arrested, stripped naked, humiliated, and condemned to die, then turned over to the Romans to be beaten.

Jesus's skin was made doubly sensitive through the extreme stress he experienced in the garden so that when he was whipped and beaten, blood poured from his body. Having not slept the night before, his exhausted frame was chained to a post, where he was scourged until he was unrecognizable. The Jews said that 40 lashes would kill a man, so they gave Jesus 39. He was then given a 100-pound piece of wood and sent on a walk to the top of the mountain outside the city. People spat at him. They mocked his power. They cursed his name.

When he reached the top of the mountain, someone offered him a second cup. This wasn't the cup of God's wrath. It was a cup of wine mixed with gall. (Matt. 27:34) This drink would numb his senses and serve as a pain reliever. It would make things easier on Jesus. This was the cup of self-preservation. The cup of convenience. It's a cup that is offered to every person in life. It tempts us to take the easy road, avoid suffering, and look out for ourselves. But Jesus wouldn't drink from that cup.

Instead, at the same place where Abraham offered his son, Isaac, and Moses met God at the burning bush, Jesus was nailed to a cross and hoisted up above the city. He was the true Isaac—the son who needed to be sacrificed—and he was the ram caught in the thicket that traded places with us. He was the Great I Am who met Moses on the same mountain, and he was the true Moses who would set his people free. Jesus, the answer to every story in Scripture, was drinking the cup of God's wrath on the cross.

Crucifixion was strategically designed by the Persians, then perfected by the Romans to maximize suffering in death. The position of the victim causes the lungs to collapse, the heart to beat faster, and carbon dioxide levels in the body to rise. The arms and wrists are dislocated, and soon the victim begins to suffocate on his own blood. Over the period of several hours, the combination of an increased heart rate, a lack of oxygen, collapsing lungs, and dehydration can lead to what is known as cardiac rupture. The heart of the victim bursts in his chest.

God the Son took on human flesh, lived a perfect life as our representative, chose to drink the cup of God's wrath, and experienced the most excruciating death as a payment for the sin of the world. And he died of a broken heart.

But the physical pain that Jesus experienced was only a fraction of his torment. It paled in comparison to the pain in his soul. Sin wreaks havoc in the soul, and sin is the root of all fear, rage, lust, and shame. Consider for a moment the last time you did something you were ashamed to admit. Remember the regret? The remorse? The vacuum in your chest that made you feel like you couldn't breathe? Do you remember the look in the eyes of your spouse or your best friend when they discovered that you let them down? Have you ever been haunted by a sense of guilt?

Sin in the soul causes immeasurable pain, yet God somehow collected all this pain and stored it in his cup of wrath. The pain of the rape victim, and the torment and guilt of the perpetrator. The pain of the abused child, and the broken heart of a divorced woman. Try to imagine all the torment of the soul compounded by millions of broken lives.

The cup of God's wrath had in it all the pain of all the sin of all those who Christ came to redeem. Like one giant nuclear bomb, God bundled all the molecules and atoms of soul-suffering into the heart of Christ and detonated it. Jesus experienced the full pain of sin on the cross when he became sin for us. This thought is beyond comprehension.

But there is an even greater pain. Humanity was created for union with God, and God is an eternal community within himself. Father, Son, and Spirit, the triune God has existed for all time in relationship with one another. On the cross, Jesus was abandoned by his friends, disowned by his community, and stripped naked by his enemies. But the greatest pain came when he was forsaken by his Father in heaven. Only in this instance on the cross does Jesus refer to the Father as "my God." (Mark 15:34) In every other instance, he calls out "my Father." Jesus changes titles because there was a change in relationship. Intimacy was lost. Connection was lost. Here on the cross, the Eternal Father turned his back on his one and only Son.

Somehow, in the cosmic mystery of the Trinity, Jesus was left abandoned and alone, and the Son of God became the object of God's intense wrath and hatred toward sin. This is the essence of hell itself in all its torment, and Jesus drank the cup of wrath until it was empty.

He embraced the first cup that would seal his fate. He rejected the second cup that would numb the pain. And he did it so that he could offer the third cup to you and me.

> And he took a cup, and when he had given thanks, he gave it to them, saying, "Drink of it, all of you, for this is my blood of the covenant, which is poured out for many for the forgiveness of sins." (Matt. 26:27–28)

The invisible God became a man so that he could shed his blood for the sins of the world, and there is enough life in his blood to wash away every sin you have ever committed or will ever commit. By placing your faith in Christ, you are fully forever forgiven of sin. We can't add anything to what he has done. We can't contribute our good deeds to our own salvation. Salvation can only come one way.

> Having forgiven us all our trespasses, by canceling the record of debt that stood against us with its legal demands. This he set aside, nailing it to the cross. (Col. 2:13–14)

All our trespasses? I remember the first time that phrase washed over me and ran through me. *All our trespasses.* What a marvel! What a mystery! The sins I committed in my darkest moments and the sins I may commit on some future day—all washed away and forgiven by the powerful blood of Jesus Christ! He was rejected by the Father so that I can be sure that I will never be rejected! He was abandoned on the cross so that I will never be abandoned or forsaken! He suffered and died so that I will never taste death even when my body expires!

Why would God do this for you and me? He doesn't need us. What would compel him to go to the cross? The answer is so pure, and so simple, and so profound.

Love. Only love.

Let it get in your bones. "We have come to know and to believe the love that God has for us." (1 John 4:16)

There is a great stage that exists in your mind. Every day, you walk out on the stage and perform. Every day, you hope that the ache in your soul for approval will find its satisfaction. And all along, everything you have ever wanted and needed has been waiting for you at the cross.

Approval. Acceptance. Hope.

We obsess over what others think because we are unsure what the Father thinks. The cross of Jesus makes it plain. You don't have to wonder anymore. He *loves* you. And he sees you without your sin. Only believe.

In him, we have redemption through his blood, the forgiveness of sins, in accordance with the riches of God's grace that he lavished on us. With all wisdom and understanding, he made known to us the mystery of his will according to his good pleasure, which he purposed in Christ. (Eph 1:7–9 NIV)

DISCUSSION QUESTIONS

1. Every person has an internal need for approval. Think about your life. Where have you recognized this need for approval in your relationships? How has a need for approval been unhealthy in your life?

2. When we don't have a complete view of our own identity, the natural inclination is to compare ourselves with others. In your

family, education, skill set, and work environment, who have you compared yourself with? What has God revealed to you about this tendency toward comparisons?

3. Every insecurity is rooted in an uncertainty of the Father's love. Spending daily time with God reading Scripture and praying, belonging to community, worshipping, and serving in the local church can help pave the way for a greater revelation of God's incredible love. What do you sense God encouraging you to do in order to live more in his love? What changes will you make this week to cooperate with what God is saying to you?

4. Which of the "two thieves" do you more readily identify with? Is it religion that pushes us to work for God's love or is it relativism, which adjusts God's standards to fit our way of living? After reflecting on the true redemption found in Christ, discuss what thought or behavior patterns need to change in your life.

5. What is the most life-changing truth you have discovered about atonement? Why did this impact you so deeply?

4

Justification

Therefore, since we have been justified by faith, we have peace with God through our Lord Jesus Christ.

—*Romans 5:1*

I knew people who had traveled to Africa. I'd seen movies about Africa explaining African culture. I had watched documentaries on various aspects of life in Africa. I'd read books on the history of nations in Africa. I had a number of close friends who grew up in Africa. But I'd never been to Africa.

Until I got on a plane in 2014 and landed in Africa, my feet had never actually walked on African earth. The pictures, the stories, the friends, and the movies were all helpful, but none of them fully prepared me for the experience of Africa. To wander the markets and chit chat with the locals. To watch the sun rise through the hills and feel the red, dusty earth between my toes. To hold the hand of an orphaned child and sneak up close to a hippopotamus in its natural environment. Africa is a land that must be experienced.

Since I was a kid, I have believed that the huge continent called Africa is a real place. I have no disputes with its existence. But believing that a certain place exists and experiencing that place yourself—those are two very different things.

For many of us, the biblical concept of justification is a lot like Africa. We believe it exists. We've heard preachers use the word, and we've noticed it in the writings of the New Testament. You could say we've seen the pictures and watched the movies, and we are sure that justification is a beautiful place on the map of Christianity.

But have you ever been there personally? Have you gotten off the airplane, left your home behind, and built a new life on the continent of justification? Do you have secondhand knowledge from a friend or a book, or do you have experiential knowledge as someone who has been there? Have you ever wandered the markets of righteousness and watched the sun rise over your insecurities? Has justification become a personal, practical, transformative revelation to you?

What does it mean to be justified? In his letter to the Romans, the apostle Paul tells us that "all have sinned and fall short of the glory of God, and are justified by his grace as a gift, through the redemption that is in Christ Jesus." (Rom. 3:23–24) We read that and often think, "Okay, justification is basically like forgiveness. This Scripture means that we are sinners, and Jesus came and died for our sins to forgive us, right?"

Right … sort of. Well, not really.

As we examined in the last chapter, Jesus certainly did die to forgive us, but forgiveness and justification are not the same. To be forgiven means you did something wrong, you went to the person and acknowledged your failure, and they have chosen to no longer hold that failure against you. But is that what *justified* means?

Think about Justin Timberlake's debut solo album in 2002. He was a young kid who had just broken off his relationship with Britney Spears and was in the process of leaving the boy band NSYNC. There are 13 songs on the album, and none of them carried this name, but he chose to name the record *Justified*. Do you think by choosing that name JT meant, "I'm sorry for the wrong things I've done. Please accept me back?" I don't think so.

Justified doesn't mean forgiven. It means "proven right." It means that the evidence proves me innocent and everything in my life lines up. You remember in school in computer lab when the teacher taught you about the word *justification*? You had to use those little buttons at the top of the word processing program that line up all the words you wrote. You can make your paragraph right-justified, left-justified, or center-justified. Whatever you choose, to be justified means that *all the words line up in a certain way.*

Think about justification in terms of a courtroom. If a man is accused of a crime and the evidence clearly shows that he committed the crime, the judge is justified in sending the man to prison. His justification is found in the evidence. If the evidence does not convict the man, then the judge is justified in releasing the accused.

When you start to understand the concept of justification, you realize that being justified is at the core of much of our day-to-day activity. Are you looking for a new job? What will you create? A résumé. A résumé is functionally your performance record, which validates or *justifies* your worth to that company. When you hand it to a potential employer you are telling them, "See, I am justified in asking for this job."

If you want to get into a prestigious university after high school, you are expected to send the university your academic record. What did you score on your SAT? How many advanced placement classes did you take? What extracurricular activities did you participate in? What was your grade-point average? That record will determine if you're good enough to get into that university. It will justify your existence there.

This is real life. It's written in the code of our DNA, and it's how we think about everything. In fact, it's the basis for every religion on Earth. Rather than bringing your academic record or your record of work performance, you naturally bring your moral record to God. We imagine that he reviews it, compares it with other applications, and then gives you access or denies you access based on your record. Some variation of that thought is the underlying premise of every religion that's ever existed: Greeks,

Persians, Hindus, Muslims, and the others. Every religion requires that you bring your record to God, and God accepts you or denies you on the basis of that record. Every religion, that is, except one.

Christianity introduced to the world a radically alien concept. In fact, it's so counterintuitive that many professing Christians run right past it and revert to building an impressive moral résumé for God. It's this fundamental misstep that is draining the joy out of the gospel for so many of us. But before we can clearly see the astonishing reality of justification, we must clearly see ourselves.

A Look in the Mirror

In the Old Testament, God reveals to his people what theologians call the moral law. These can be summed up in the Ten Commandments. You shall have no other gods before me, you shall not worship an idol, or take God's name in vain. Remember the Sabbath, honor your parents, do not commit murder, adultery, steal or lie. Do not covet.

A brief, honest examination of the moral law will uncover the reality that you and I have broken every one of these commands in our hearts. We've valued money, relationships, and status above God at various times, and we've idolized sex or power or certain possessions. We've overworked and ignored God's plan for rest and have dishonored our parents. Jesus said to hate someone is murder in your heart and to look lustfully is adultery. We've stolen and lied about it, and we've jealously wanted things that weren't ours.

In fact, sin has so often ruled in our hearts that God is the one who is justified in saying, "By works of the law, no human being will be justified in his sight." (3:20) To deeply understand justification, we must first realize that our case before God is absolutely hopeless! You are not one or two notches away from acceptable before a holy and perfect God. You are light years away! Your sin may seem small and even *justifiable* to you, but God, who is perfect, makes it clear that no human being will ever be justified by their own works in his sight.

It's not enough, however, just to see your sinfulness. You also have to come to terms with the fact that you can't fix the situation. No amount of good deeds or payment on your part could ever remove the debt. God is the Eternal Judge of all creation. He will stand over everyone and everything as a righteous judge. In the Book of Revelation, John describes the coming judgment of God like this:

> And I saw a great white throne and the one sitting on it. The earth and sky fled from his presence, but they found no place to hide. I saw the dead, both great and small, standing before God's throne. And the books were opened, including the Book of Life. And the dead were judged according to what they had done, as recorded in the books. (Rev. 20:11–12 NLT)

God is so holy and perfect that even the earth and sky flee in fear of his holiness. Your moral record will then be held up before the perfectly holy and just God on the Day of Judgment. If you're like me, you agree that is a terrifying thought.

Forgiveness before God is a legal pardon on the day of my trial. It would be the equivalent of the judge saying, "Your bail has been posted, your debt has been paid, you are free to go." The gospel claims that forgiveness is available to all who believe, because of the shed blood of Jesus on the cross. That's gloriously incredible news. But that's not where it ends. "Since we have been justified by faith, we have peace with God." (Rom. 5:1)

Justification is more than the removal of debt; it's the bestowal of status. It's not just having your bail posted. It's walking out of jail and being driven to a grand ballroom where guests await you. You're ushered up to the stage, and it's announced that you are the recipient of the Nobel Prize. They put a massive gold medal around your neck and a hefty check in your hand. For the rest of your life, you are a part of the small, prestigious group of highly honored individuals. You are invited to private functions, given honor everywhere you go, and given access into a powerful circle of relationships. You've not just been forgiven; you've been justified.

How could the New Testament claim that sinful people are justified before God? How could my record be seen as worthy of honor? Doesn't the Bible teach that to acquit the guilty and condemn the innocent is detestable to the Lord (Prov. 17:15)? How could God see me as righteous and still be just?

Trading Places

In 1881, Mark Twain published his first well-known historical fiction novel titled *The Prince and the Pauper.*[1] It's the story of two boys who meet by chance in the courtyard outside the palace in London. One boy is Tom Canty, a poor young man living with his abusive father. The other is Prince Edward, son of the king and future ruler of England. The two realize that they share a strong resemblance in appearance and decide to trade places. Edward puts on Tom's rags, and Tom puts on Edward's robes. Soon, Edward is being mistreated in the slums of the city, and Tom is being honored and celebrated in the halls of the palace.

The story ends when Edward resumes his rightful place, and Tom is celebrated for his humble willingness to step down. I can remember reading this story as a kid and being fascinated by the plot. Imagine what it was like for Tom Canty, trading places with the prince. Everything in his life changed in a moment. One minute, his opinion meant nothing to anyone, and the next minute he was making judgments of national importance! One minute, he only owned the clothes on his back, and the next minute, the nation's greatest treasures were at his disposal! This type of instantaneous repositioning stirs something deep inside us, because it is the echo of an even more amazing truth:

God made him who had no sin to be sin for us, so that in him
we might become the righteousness of God. (2 Cor. 5:21 NIV)

Theologians call this double imputation. When the Son of God, the
Prince of Heaven, came to Earth in human form, he came to put on the
rags of Tom Canty. He came to be mistreated in the streets of the city
and to identify with the rejection of humanity. But he came for so much
more. When Jesus died on the cross and drank the cup of God's wrath
for us, he received the judgment that we deserve. *God made him who had
no sin to be sin for us,* but the exchange went both ways! Christ stood in
the courtroom of eternity as if he were you, so that now, you can stand
before God forever as if you were Christ! Meditate for a moment on the
second half of 2 Corinthians 5:21. *In him we might become—the righteousness of God!*

To "impute" means *to think of as belonging to.* It means *to consider it
so.* God thinks of your sins—past, present and future, as having been
transferred into Christ's account, and he thinks of Christ's righteous
record, his perfect life, his spotless obedience—as being transferred
into your account. This means that when God sees you, he chooses to
see the perfect righteous record of his Son in place of your imperfect
life! He imputes that record to you and declares that you're not only
forgiven, you are perfect!

This sounds like madness! It sounds too good to be true! In fact, it's
too good *not* to be true. No human being would ever create a gospel like
this. Theologian Richard Hooker once said, "Let it be counted folly, or
frenzy, or fury whatsoever, it is our comfort and our wisdom; that we
care for no knowledge in the world but this, that man hath sinned, and
God hath suffered; that God hath made himself the son of man, and that
men are made the righteousness of God."[2]

It may sound like folly or frenzy. It may sound like foolishness. But
look closer! Let your heart drink deeply of this truth. In the midst of your

half-successful attempts to please God, he has already decided that your record is perfect before him! The writer of the Book of Hebrews puts it like this:

For by a single offering, he has perfected for all time those who are being sanctified. (Heb. 10:14)

Did you catch the tension? You and I are still in the middle of the process of change. We haven't arrived. At times, we are still selfish, and fearful, and lustful, and proud. Yet while God is working on us from the inside out, he has already perfected us for all time through a single offering! Notice the timing of it all. The process of holiness takes a lifetime, but the imputation of righteousness is instantaneous! In other words, the moment you trust in Christ, repent, and turn to God—at that very moment—the perfect, spotless record of Jesus is yours, and you can never be cursed by God again! He emptied his judgment for sin on Jesus at the cross so that today there is no judgment left for you! The only thing he has left is the blessing due his Son, and that blessing now belongs to you!

Justification is an instantaneous legal act performed by the Judge. He swung the gavel. He spoke the decree. *It is finished.* Theologian J. I. Packer writes, "Nobody can produce new evidence of your depravity that will make God change his mind. For God justified you with (so to speak) his eyes open. He knew the worst about you at the time when he accepted you for Jesus' sake; and the verdict which he passed then was, and is, final."[3]

In the American court system, we have something called double jeopardy. (This has nothing to do with Alex Trebek, I promise.) It's a law that protects the accused of being tried for the same crime on the same evidence. Once you are acquitted, no one can accuse you again. With God, the evidence of your life is already in. He sees the beginning and the end. He knows how long you will live, and every sin you will ever commit. When Christ died on the cross, he paid for every sin, and when God made his decree, it was final. You can never be condemned. You can never be accused. "There is therefore, now, no condemnation for those who are in Christ Jesus!" (Rom 8:1) Theologian and pastor John Piper put it this way:

> Christ fulfilled all righteousness perfectly; and then that righteousness was reckoned to be mine, when I trusted in him. I was counted righteous. God looked on Christ's perfect righteousness and he declared me to be righteous with the righteousness of Christ.[4]

This means that repentance isn't just about sin. When most of us think of repentance, we think of saying that we're sorry for sins we've committed, but this isn't really the full meaning. Repentance is abandoning all trust in anyone or anything other than Jesus. When I repent, I turn from sin, because I realize that it offends a holy God and destroys my soul. But I also repent of my own righteousness. All my inner attempts to self-justify, all my inner dialogue to excuse certain failures or behaviors, all the evidence I've been saving up to convince myself and my friends, and ultimately God, that I'm really a good person—all of it must be burned! Let it go! Run from it! Christ has performed the great exchange and I cannot earn this position through my efforts! I can only receive this position *by faith.*

"Therefore, since we have been justified by faith, we have peace with God through our Lord Jesus Christ." (5:1) Justified by faith? Not tears? Not prayers? Not works? Just faith. Sometimes we have a tendency to overcomplicate a brutally simple invitation. Faith is not some mysterious, ambiguous force in the universe. Faith is simply reliance or confidence in someone or something.

I have faith in my wife to prepare dinner tonight. I have faith in my car to start when I turn the key. Some things in life are reliable, while other things I should question. To be justified by faith simply means that the object of my faith, namely Jesus, is absolutely reliable, and I have decided to fully lean on his reliability.

Yet there is this tendency in all of us to resist absolute dependence on anyone. I feel it, for example, every time I board an airplane. I don't know the first thing about aviation or the science of flight, and yet when I sit on that plane and buckle in, I often feel the need to somehow contribute to the flight's success. I find myself scoping out the wing through my window and wondering, *Are all those flaps supposed to be there? It seems to be moving in a strange way.* Or *I think I heard a troubling sound in the air system. Maybe there's a problem with the oxygen flow.*

Something in me doesn't like being fully dependent on the pilot and the crew. If they mess up, we're all dead, and those odds make me a bit uncomfortable. It would be ridiculous if, as the flight was taking off, I lifted my body off of my chair in an attempt to help the pilot get us off the ground. I don't have anything to contribute. I need to come to terms with that. I should sit back, order a Coke, and eat the pretzels.

Since we have been justified by faith, we must each embrace the reality that we cannot contribute to our own justification. It must be received freely, and fully, and when we receive it this way, the results are guaranteed: *peace with God.*

This is how justification becomes experiential knowledge. It's the difference between seeing pictures of Africa and moving to Africa. You know that justification has taken root in your heart when the peace of God rules in your soul. Then there is no more posturing, no more striving, and no more straining. A confident reliance on Jesus fundamentally changes the way the believer approaches God.

Years ago, when the truth of justification first began to rattle my soul, I stumbled upon this quote from the nineteenth-century preacher Charles Spurgeon:

Let us remember how near we really are. We have been washed from every sin in the precious blood of Jesus; we are covered from head to foot at this moment with the spotless righteousness of Immanuel, God with us; we are accepted in the Beloved; yea, we are at this moment one with Christ, and members of his body. How could we be nearer? How near is Christ to God? So near are we! Come near, then, in your personal pleadings, for you are near in your covenant representative. The Lord Jesus has taken manhood into union with the divine nature, and now between God and man there exists a special and unparalleled relationship, the likes of which the universe cannot present. Come near, O ye sons of God, come near, for you are near.[5]

Read it again. One more time, if you would. I read and reread that quote literally hundreds of times. It was through that simple paragraph that the truth of justification finally dawned on my soul. Like waves of glory breaking in my heart, I finally began to see what the early Christians were so excited about. How near can I come to God?

"Let us go right into the presence of God with sincere hearts fully trusting him." (Heb. 10:22 NLT) I can come as near to God as Jesus the Son can come? I have unhindered access to God? Could this really be?

How powerful are my prayers if I pray confident in my justification? "Very truly I tell you, my Father will give you whatever you ask in my name. Until now, you have not asked for anything in my name. Ask and you will receive, and your joy will be complete." (John 16:23–24 NIV) My prayers are as powerful as if they were uttered from the mouth of Jesus himself! It's no wonder Jesus says that my joy will be made complete! He gave me his name, he gave me his access, he gave me his record! But more than any of these precious gifts, the greatest of these is love. He gave me *his* love.

"I am in them and you are in me. May they experience such perfect unity that the world will know that you sent me and that you love them as much as you love me." (John 17:23 NLT) Consider this: God the Father in heaven loves me with the same perfect love that he has eternally had for the Son. He can do this because he sees the Son in me. I am in Christ, and Christ is in me. Through faith in Christ, I am invited into intimate relationship with the Trinity, Father, Son, and Spirit, in an eternal unbroken love relationship. And now, those who have been justified by faith participate in that relationship forever.

When Jesus touched the leper or honored his parents or was baptized in the Jordan or showed compassion to the little children—every righteous deed Jesus ever performed—they were all credited to me. By faith in Christ, I receive the righteous record of Christ. All his good works on Earth made him perfect, and his perfect standing is now mine. God accepts me according to Christ's record rather than my own.

Jesus has not simply given me peace. He has traded places with me, taken my sin on himself, and given me his perfect record before God. He has given me *his* peace.

> Peace I leave with you; my peace I give to you. Not as the world gives do I give to you. Let not your hearts be troubled, neither let them be afraid. (John 14:27)

Total victory over fear comes when we deeply internalize justification by faith. I have perfect peace because I have access to the peace of Jesus, and he is perfect. The Hebrew word for peace is *shalom*. It means "nothing missing and nothing lacking." It is more than the absence of war. It is the presence of God. This is what Christ has made available to all those who repent of their sin, repent of their righteousness, and believe the good news of grace. He drank all of God's cup of wrath. Why would we hesitate to drink all of his cup of grace?

DISCUSSION QUESTIONS

1. What stood out to you most in this chapter? What was confusing? What was helpful?

2. What comes into your mind when you hear the word *justified*? What does this word mean to you? How did this chapter impact your understanding of what it means biblically to be justified?

3. Human nature craves justification. It's why we work hard on our résumés and our GPAs. We desire to prove our worth. This is the basis for every major religion except Christianity. We hope to gain access to God based on our moral goodness. Talk about your experience with this sort of mindset. Did you grow up needing to prove yourself? How did you carry that into adulthood?

4. Read 2 Corinthians 5:21. The biblical truth of justification is revolutionary and goes against the grain of our human nature. Jesus not only purchased your forgiveness, but he imputed his perfect, righteousness record to your account. You're not just forgiven; God sees you as perfect in Christ. How do you think your life would be different if you fully believed this truth?

5

Adoption

And behold, a voice from heaven said, "This is my beloved Son, with whom I am well pleased."

—Matthew 3:17

On December 4, 1972, seven-year-old Steven Stayner was walking home from school when he was approached by a man and invited into the man's car.[1] Steven agreed and didn't see his family again until he was 14. In those seven years of abuse and deception, Steven Stayner lost track of his identity. He couldn't remember who he was, who his family was, what his birthday was, or where he lived. In the police report the day he was rescued, his testimony read, "I don't know my true birthdate...I know my first name is Steven." That's all he had left.

There are countless horrible tragedies in this world, but nothing cuts to the heart like a child ripped from his family. Family is supposed to be a safe place. It's the protective environment where we each discover our strengths and weaknesses, explore our interests, and confront our fears. It's the place where we develop a sense of personal identity and value and purpose.

Family helps us answer millions of questions that we often don't even realize we're asking. We learn our ethnicity, we develop our eating preferences, we are taught how to handle conflict. And when everyone else abandons us, there's still family. Musician Nathan Feuerstein, in his song "I Can Feel It," writes:

> "Records stop selling, these people won't care for me. The older I get, the more family is everything."[2]

It's true. Family is everything. Unless of course, your family is falling apart.

In today's world, few people can honestly say that *family* is a place of safety and joy. Most of us have a collection of stepbrothers and half sisters and broken marriages and unsettled issues. Even in healthy families with parents who love each other, chaos and pain are still present. Tragically, rather than being a place of stability, family is often ground zero for instability.

When I was in college, one of my closest friends received a phone call from his mom where she told him that his father was not his biological dad. I stood next to my friend and watched as his entire world crumbled around him. His dad wasn't *his* dad? Who was his dad, then? And who was this other guy who had been his dad five minutes ago? And what about his brother? That person wasn't his actual brother? Before the phone call, my friend was half Jamaican. He had learned Jamaican culture and embraced this as part of his identity. Now what was he?

Interestingly enough, a quick survey of the Scriptures won't bring much hope to the idea of family stability. Cain killed his brother Abel, Jacob deceived his brother Esau, Isaac played favorites with his kids, Judah slept with his son's wife, David's son raped his sister, and on and on. Brokenness, dysfunction, and pain. If family is so necessary for our well-being and yet so broken in our experience, where do we turn? We want to feel like we're home. We want to feel like we're safe. We want to feel like someone cares, and we belong, and someone is going to look out for us. But tragically, many of us just feel alone.

Psychologists tell us that loneliness is at an all-time high in our culture. We are more connected through technology, yet more lonely and disconnected at the same time. Have you ever turned on the TV at your house or the radio on in your car, just to break the silence and have some company? I admit I have. We don't know how to be alone because we don't know how to deal with the loneliness on the inside. If family is everything, how does family really work? What's the deeper truth that redeems and restores the duct-tape version of family that we actually experience?

So far, we've learned how Jesus takes our sins through the atonement. Through justification, Jesus takes our place. But it's through adoption that Jesus takes our "aloneness." That deep inner sense telling you that you are alone, that no one is listening, and that no one is looking out for you—that cavern created by your inevitably imperfect family—can actually be filled once and for all by Jesus. But how?

Spiritual Adoption

The word *adoption* is first introduced in the New Testament by the apostle Paul in his letter to the Romans. He writes:

> For you did not receive the spirit of slavery to fall back into fear,
> but you have received the Spirit of adoption as sons, by whom
> we cry "Abba! Father!" (Rom. 8:15)

The word *adoption* carries with it a legal connotation. It's an agreement that is signed and recognized by law. When an orphan needs a home, and someone who is not the natural parent takes on the full responsibility of the parent, this is called adoption. Part of what Jesus accomplished through his life, death, and resurrection was your legal adoption into his eternal family. The adoption is legal because it's recognized in the courtroom of God, the Great Judge, and it's eternal because you are adopted into God's family. Many theologians regard adoption as the most sacred and special aspect of the gospel exchange because it reveals something unique about God.

You were born a sinner. But he came and *chose* you.

Often when we think of adoption, we think of it as Plan B. Children are put up for adoption when their parents have abandoned them. Families often adopt if they're unable to have kids. Our natural inclination is to think that God chose to adopt us because his Plan A failed. Interestingly enough, we are told in the Scriptures that that's not the case. What seems like Plan B in the natural was actually always God's Plan A. He knew about sin and death before Adam ever chose rebellion. And in his infinite wisdom, God allowed the drama of human history to play out, always preparing you for adoption.

> In love, he predestined us for adoption to himself as sons through Jesus Christ, according to the purpose of his will to the praise of his glorious grace. (Eph. 1:4–6)

Did you catch that? Predestined. He saw the garden, sin, rebellion—everything. Before any of it had happened, God chose to adopt us. Why? *To the praise of his glorious grace.* He always planned to use adoption to display his nature and reveal his glory. He could have done this in countless ways, but nothing shines quite like adoption. Nothing is quite as beautiful. Adoption reveals to us something unique and compelling about the God of the universe. He didn't just love us because we were his biological kids. He chose us. And like every adoption, it was complicated and costly.

In his letter to the Romans, Paul contrasts adoption with what he calls "the spirit of slavery." This illustration would have resonated with first-century Christians in a profound way. The Roman Empire at the time was home to millions of slaves. One out of every three people alive was a slave. You and I have probably never actually met a slave in real life, but everyone in the first-century church had met one, and many who were reading Paul's letters were themselves slaves.

And slavery in Rome was ugly. As a slave, you couldn't vote. You couldn't testify in court. You could be raped or beaten or abused or killed without any recourse. You were the property of your owner and there was no accountability. The position of the slave was one of utter despair. Like Steven Stayner trapped in the home of his kidnapper, the slave had lost all sense of his identity. He couldn't make his own choices or pursue his own interests, and his position was hopeless.

Paul, however, tells us that at its core slavery is not just an external condition. Though the external condition of slavery is abominable, the internal condition, or the *spirit of slavery*, is far worse. It does not just affect one out of every three in ancient Rome. It affects one hundred out of one hundred in every generation. Slavery is the spiritual condition of broken humanity.

Much Afraid

We are told that a spirit of slavery causes us to fall back into fear. Wait. Back into fear? This means that *fear* is a place we've already been. Fear grows in the human heart as naturally as grass grows on the hills. We fear other people, we fear weakness, we fear lack, we fear the unknown. Every one of us has an individual set of personal fears. This may include external ones like a fear of spiders or enclosed spaces or airplanes or heights. But we also each have a set of internal fears, invisible ones, like the fear of failure or the fear of rejection or the fear of being alone. Some fears are learned, and some seem to spring up on their own, but every fear points to something bigger. Buried in the human psyche is what we could call *the Great Fear*.

You are afraid of death. And so am I.

It may not be the actual experience of death that terrifies you. The real fear of death isn't in the pain alone but in what happens after the pain. What is it going to be like? What will happen once your heart stops beating? What will happen when your body goes cold? What will you see? What will you feel?

If we're honest, most of us don't like to think about this very long. It's unknown, but whether you realize it or not, it lingers in the background of your subconscious, like the droning sound of the highway in the distance. You are going to die. And after you die...

What will it be like to stand before God? What will it be like to be judged? It's inevitable, yet we go to great lengths to avoid thinking about it. We distract ourselves with TV shows and earthly accomplishments in the hope of drowning out the roar of death in the distance. Sometimes the distractions work, and then something happens—a car accident, the loss of a friend, a bad diagnosis—and these events shake us out of the dream and remind us of reality. Death is coming. And fear lingers. But it's this deeply rooted fear that Jesus came to abolish through adoption.

> Since therefore the children share in flesh and blood, he himself likewise partook of the same things, that through death he might destroy the one who has the power of death, that is, the devil, and deliver all those who through fear of death were subject to lifelong slavery. (Heb. 2:14–15)

God's plan in Christ is to strangle this fear once and for all, to reestablish humanity on an entirely new footing. This is why Paul writes, "You did not receive the spirit of slavery to fall back into fear, but you have received the Spirit of adoption as sons." (Rom. 8:15)

You have received a new spirit. He calls it the "Spirit of adoption." Adoption in the ancient world was slightly different from what we know today. Before the birth of Christianity, there is little evidence that Greeks or Romans would adopt orphaned children simply for charity. The word *adoption* as used by Paul was typically used to describe a wealthy person who had no biological heir. They would often adopt a child or an adult and confer on them all the legal rights and privileges that would normally be given to a natural child.

Dr. Timothy Keller, quoting Francis Lyall, states: "The profound truth of Roman adoption was that the adoptee was taken out of his previous state and placed in a new relationship of son to his new father. All of his old debts were instantly canceled, and in effect, the adoptee started a new life as part of this new family. ...The new father was liable for the actions of the adoptee, and each owed the other reciprocal duties of support and maintenance."[3] Adoption was a cutting off of the old family name and establishment of a new lineage. The old debts didn't come with you! In ancient Roman culture, the law stated that a parent could disinherit a biological child, but they could not disinherit an adopted child!

Paul is trying to tell us something when he says that we have been given the *Spirit of adoption*. God has gone to great lengths so that you and I can die with assurance. Christ came to Earth to identify with humanity, he died on the cross as atonement for our sins, and he exchanged places with us to establish our legal justification. But adoption goes further than all of these. Adoption changes the relational structure between us and God. It changes the way God approaches us and the way we can approach him. Matthew Henry, in his commentary on Romans writes, "God as a Judge by the spirit of bondage sends us to Christ as Mediator, and Christ as Mediator, by the spirit of adoption, sends us back again to God as a Father."[4]

Do you see it? Has the truth dawned on your heart? It's true that God is the Judge. It's true that he is the King. It's true that he is the Creator. He is all these things. But for you and me, and all who place their faith in Christ alone, God is not any of these things *first*.

Through the gospel, your first relationship to God is Father and son.
Soak in that for a minute. Not master and servant. Not judge and
criminal. Not king and citizen—Father and son. Allow the truth of this
statement to make its way into your heart because this truth changes *everything.* Jesus said, when you pray, pray like this: "Our Father…" From
now on, every interaction you have with God is filtered through the lens
of a father and his child.

I have three sons. Recently my oldest son sang in a chorus concert
for school. Imagine 300 elementary school kids all dressed with white
shirts and black pants, packed into a gymnasium with hundreds of parents, grandparents, aunts, uncles, and teachers. As the kids began to sing
their first song, I stood in the back looking over the heads of others.
What was I looking for? Just one thing. I was looking for my boy. I didn't
mean any disrespect to the other children, but there was really only one
kid I was interested in watching that night—my son. Why? Because he's
mine. And honestly, I don't really care how well he sings or how tall he is
compared to the other kids. I just care that he's mine. Parents don't see
their kids through the same lens that they see everyone else. This is just
a fact of life. In our adoption, God tells us, "No longer do I see you as
just one person in the sea of humanity. I've chosen you and adopted you.
From now on, I see you as mine."

Allow me to use another illustration. Statistics tell us that high
school football players have a very slim chance of ever playing football in
the NCAA. Only 6.5% of high school players ever make it. That means
93.5% don't. Of that small percentage who play in college, only 1.5% will
ever suit up for an NFL game, and many who suit up will never actually play.[5] With these statistics in mind, no one was surprised when both
Peyton Manning and Eli Manning were drafted by teams in the NFL,
and both went on to win a pair of Super Bowls. Why wasn't anyone
surprised? Because their father is NFL legend Archie Manning, and it
wasn't just DNA that got those boys to the highest level; it was training

and opportunity. Archie didn't treat his sons like every other kid at the chorus concert, and neither would you. And neither does God. Archie Manning gave his sons special attention. He worked with them for hours one-on-one. He opened doors for them that never would have opened if he hadn't been their father. He set them up to succeed, guided them at every stage of development, and counseled them along the way. He did all this because Peyton and Eli are *his* kids.

So what are the implications of adoption? What does it mean to actually be a child of God? Theologian J. I. Packer writes:

> Our understanding of Christianity cannot be better than our grasp of adoption. ...If you want to judge how well a person understands Christianity, find out how much he makes of the thought of being God's child and having God as his Father. If this is not the thought that prompts and controls his worship and prayers and whole outlook on life, it means that he does not understand Christianity very well at all.[6]

Have you experienced freedom from fear at the very core of your being? Does the truth of adoption prompt and control your prayers and your overall outlook on life? It should, and it could, but it will take some rewiring. You must retrain your heart to make your first instinct "Abba, Father."

The Experience of Sonship

In his first great literary achievement, late-night talk-show host Jimmy Fallon wrote a children's book titled *Your Baby's First Word Will Be Dada*.[7] The book shows several different animal dads trying to get their babies to say, "Dada." Each time, the baby makes its natural animal sound instead. So the baby cow says "Moo" and the baby duck says "Quack." The dads are frustrated and can't seem to get their children to comply. One by one, the children continue to make the sound that comes most naturally to them. The baby horse says "Neigh" and the baby frog says "Ribbit." Finally, on the very last page of the book, with one last attempt, all the fathers plead with their children, and the children erupt with a ground-shaking "DADA."

My youngest son loves the book, and I couldn't get it out of my mind as I wrote this chapter on adoption. Right now, God's Spirit calls to us saying, "Look to God as Father," yet so often we respond with the sound that comes most naturally to us. "Lord," we say. "Master. King." He looks back and says, "First, Dada." This is the revelation of adoption, but some broken part of our hearts resists it. We are more comfortable thinking about God as our ruler. We are more comfortable thinking about God as our judge. Still his Spirit calls to each of us saying, "If you want to truly know me, your first word must be Dada...this is our primary relationship."

In the story of the prodigal son, when the youngest son seeks to return to his dad, he doesn't ask to be reinstated as a son. He asks instead to be treated like a hired worker. I can relate to this. There is something in me that would rather interact with God in an employer/employee relationship. It's safer and cleaner, and I can go back to my own home at the end of the day.

To call him Father means that he lives in the home we go back to. He's at every holiday and family function. He's involved in every aspect of our lives, and this can be intimidating. I remember hearing one scholar call this tendency to resist God's love "the prodigal's suspicion."[8] It's difficult for us to accept the idea that we have been welcomed by God. The younger son in the story received the robe and the ring and the sandals, but it still wasn't enough to convince him of the father's intentions! Something in him resisted the father's acceptance. So the Scripture adds, "And he [the father] ran and embraced him and kissed him [fervently]." (Luke 15:20 AMPC)

The text implies not one kiss, but many. You and I need more than the legal status of sons. We need more than signed paperwork. We need the experience of sons: the frequent embrace and kiss of the Father. This is why God sent forth his Spirit. Paul outlines it like this in his letter to the Galatians:

> But when the fullness of time had come, God sent forth his Son, born of woman, born under the law, to redeem those who were under the law, so that we might receive adoption as sons. (Gal. 4:4–5)

Follow the train of thought here: God sent Jesus into the world to redeem us and purchase *sonship*. This secures our legal status as adopted children of God, but the text doesn't stop there.

> And because you are sons, God has sent the Spirit of his Son into our hearts, crying, "Abba! Father!" (4:6)

God doesn't just want us to have the legal status of adoption; he wants us to have the inner experience of adoption. So he sends his Son into the world to purchase our sonship, then he sends his Spirit into our hearts to convince us of sonship. In other words, you can know the inner experience of adoption yourself right now! His Spirit within your heart is seeking to teach you a new word: *Abba*. The word means "Daddy" or even "Dada." It's the personal, intimate, simple expression of a child toward his father. In every situation, God wants this to be the first word on your lips, because *through the gospel, your first relationship to God is Father and son.*

Keller, in his book on prayer, recounts the following story:

> Thomas Goodwin, a seventeenth-century Puritan pastor, wrote that once he saw a father and son walking along the street. Suddenly, the father swept the son up into his arms and hugged

him and kissed him and told the boy he loved him—and then after a minute, he put the boy back down. Was the little boy more a son in the father's arms than he was down on the street? Objectively and legally, there was no difference, but subjectively and experientially, there was all the difference in the world. In his father's arms, the boy was experiencing his sonship.[9]

I think that this is the essence of what the apostle John meant when he wrote, "We have come to know and to believe the love that God has for us." (1 John 4:16) I don't just mentally agree with it. I don't just cerebrally know it. Beyond intellectual understanding, there is an experiential reality. Adoption provides the actual framework for intimate communion with God.

In my personal journey of faith, this is where the ground is most sacred. This is where I hesitate to write, because some things just cannot be written. Charles Austin Miles caught the fragrance of this truth when he wrote the famous hymn "In the Garden."

And he walks with me. And he talks with me. And he tells me I am his own. And the joy we share as we tarry there, none other has ever known.[10]

There must be a secret communion with God. There must be a meeting place of the soul. On the backside of the desert, where no other voice can reach you, Father and son commune. It's only in this sacred place that fear can be wrestled to the ground and overcome—when the voice of God speaks through the Spirit of God, and your soul finds a deep assurance that you really are a child of God.

And behold, a voice from heaven said, "This is my beloved Son, with whom I am well pleased." (Matt. 3:17)

It's in this place that the striving can finally cease. The need to prove yourself is extinguished. The need to compete with others to validate your own worth no longer claws at your heart. All the needs of your soul that *family* sought to provide—the security, the significance, the sense of identity—God provides through the Spirit of adoption. Confidence, assurance, courage, endurance—they all find their source in the Spirit of adoption. Pastor and author T. D. Jakes writes, "A person who comprehends that they are accepted in the beloved is a person who has all the acceptance he will ever need."[11]

Maybe the old preacher Charles Spurgeon wasn't exaggerating when he called the gospel essential wisdom: enthroned, crowned, and glorified. Maybe everything the soul longs for can actually be discovered here. Because adoption doesn't just heal the soul; adoption brings with it inheritance.

The Privileges of Sons

You may be wondering why the Scripture keeps specifically referring to sons. What about daughters? Don't these truths apply to both men and women? If so, why does Scripture keep calling Christians "sons of God"? The Bible makes it clear that our relationship to God through Christ transcends our ethnicity, our heritage, and even our gender (Gal. 3:28). In other words, before you are a man or a woman or a Jew or a Gentile, your core identity is a child of God. But in the ancient world, not all children were treated the same. Specifically, the first-born son was given the greatest inheritance and the privilege of carrying the family name. Just as both men and women in the Bible are called "the Bride of Christ," (so guys, you're the bride too!), both men and women are given the inheritance of the *sons of God*. Scripture is using a cultural practice to teach us a spiritual truth. Paul refers to us as sons, so that we understand that our position includes an inheritance.

So you are no longer a slave, but a son, and if a son, then an heir through God. (4:7)

God has prepared an eternal inheritance for you, purchased for you through the cross. It's not something you earn or deserve. An inheritance is something that is freely given by a parent to a child. The wealthier the parents are, the greater the inheritance. But what does God have in store for his children? What inheritance could the Maker of all things possibly give us?

No eye has seen, no ear has heard, and no mind has imagined what God has prepared for those who love him. (1 Cor. 2:9 NLT)

We can't even begin to comprehend. Any attempt to quantify the future inheritance of the saints only scratches the surface. Your imagination cannot reach the heights of God's reality. So let your heart hope; his plan of blessing is immeasurably greater than your greatest desire.

We can, however, see some of the outer edges of our inheritance. First, we see that God provides for our hearts what *family* always intended to provide. In Christ, we find perfect protection.

"But the Lord is faithful, and he will strengthen and protect you from the evil one." (2 Thes. 3:3 NASB) This doesn't mean that bad things will never happen to Christians, but it does mean that evil never wins in the Christian's life. Through hardship, struggle, loss, and pain, God always turns things around for our good and his glory (Rom. 8:28). He always leads us in triumph (2 Cor. 2:14) and protects us from the plans of the enemy. Just as a father protects his family, the Father of spirits will always keep your spirit. Knowing this allows the adopted child of God to rest in the perfect protection of the Father. He has a plan. You don't need to entertain the fears that would try to deceive you.

In Christ, provision is part of our inheritance. "And if God cares so wonderfully for wildflowers that are here today and thrown into the fire tomorrow, he will certainly care for you. Why do you have so little faith? So don't worry about these things...your heavenly Father already knows all your needs. Seek the Kingdom of God above all else and live righteously, and he will give you everything you need." (Matt. 6:30–33 NLT)

Your Father knows what you need and isn't going to let his child go without. Rest in his provision, trust his wisdom. Take hold of the promise by faith. God is a Father who always works hard to make sure his kids have everything they need.

In Christ, we receive guidance. "For all who are led by the Spirit of God are sons of God." (Rom. 8:14) God will instruct you and lead you in life. He promises, like every good parent, to provide wisdom and guidance through life's biggest decisions. For every ache in your heart that *family* attempts to satisfy, God, through adoption, provides the ultimate expression.

Even in suffering, God teaches us the reality of our adoption (8:17). It's often through the hardest and most difficult times that we develop the substance of our faith. The love of God becomes real, and the promises of God take root in our hearts. Through trial, God proves to us that he never fails. Nothing will refine the soul like suffering (1 Pet. 1:6–7). And like in every healthy home, God teaches us boundaries through his loving discipline. Sometimes he takes things away, and sometimes he makes us wait. As a loving Father, God shapes his children through steady, diligent discipline (Heb. 12:7–11).

But the future inheritance goes even further. He promises eternal life, an imperishable body, and the opportunity to rule over creation with him. He promises a new heaven and a new Earth. And all of this—the provision, the protection, the guidance, the discipline, the eternal reward, and the glory—all of it points to something greater. Because the greatest thing God could give us isn't a thing at all. It's himself. There is no greater inheritance than God himself, so God gave us God as our great inheritance.

> And I heard a loud voice from the throne saying, "Behold the dwelling place of God is with man. He will dwell with them, and they will be his people and God himself will be with them as their God. He will wipe away every tear from their eyes, and death shall be no more, neither shall there be mourning nor crying, nor pain anymore, for the former things have passed away." (Rev. 21:3–4)

God promises an eternity with God. At first it may sound strange to our natural minds, but there is really no greater gift that he could give. This is the mystery of spiritual adoption. Not a slave, a son. Not a criminal before a judge, but a child before their daddy. We can actually experience the freedom of adoption when we retrain our hearts to receive his kindness and call him "Abba."

DISCUSSION QUESTIONS

1. Describe in three words the family you grew up in. What image comes to mind when you hear the word "family"? How has that changed since following Jesus?

2. Every person battles with fear in one way or another. Our adoption in Christ is God's great force to extinguish our fears. As you read this chapter, what fears in your own soul did you sense the Holy Spirit highlighting? Talk honestly about how these fears have affected your life. What is one truth from Scripture that you can embrace to silence fear?

3. When you hear the word "father," what thoughts come to mind? Seeing God as Father first means understanding that he treats you as one of his kids, rather than as a law-breaker or a stranger.

How does this view of God change the way you pray? How does it change the way you look at life?

4. God desires the experience of our adoption to go from our heads to our hearts. One of the most powerful ways this happens is to speak the truth of God's Word over our lives. Here's an example of a scriptural declaration for you from 1 John 4:16: "Today, I know—I experience and rely on—the love that God has for me. As a group, read aloud the following verses. After each verse, create declarative truths that you can pray over in your life every day. (Romans 8:15, Ephesians 1:4–6, Hebrews 2:14–15, Galatians 4:6–7)

5. One great benefit of adoption is provision. God knows and sees every need. Take some time and, in faith, pray for one another for specific needs in your life.

6

Resurrection

So, my brothers and sisters, you also died to the law through the body of Christ, that you might belong to another, to him who was raised from the dead, in order that we might bear fruit for God.

—Romans 7:4 NIV

I like snow. I like taking my boys sledding and having snowball fights in the backyard. It might sound strange, but I even like driving in the snow. However, on February 7, 2013, my generally positive relationship with snow took a sharp turn for the worst. That was the day when the six states of New England were buried in what was later called "Snowmageddon." My street got 40 inches of snow over the course of a day or two, and there was nothing anyone could do. Shops closed for days, houses lost power, and my road didn't see a plow truck on February 7, or February 8, or February 9. By the third day, I started feeling like our fine city had forgotten that our street existed.

Usually, a snow day with the kids is fun. You make a fire, drink some hot chocolate, and play board games. But by day two, I was getting restless. I wanted to see what the world looked like beyond my front door, and clearly the city plow trucks had not made our little road a priority, so I decided to take matters into my own hands. I gathered my friends and neighbors, gave a rousing speech, and convinced them that we could dig ourselves out of this.

At first it seemed ridiculous. There were only four or five of us. We had five shovels, and our snow blower broke within the first five minutes. The snow was heavy and still falling, and it didn't take long before one of the shovels snapped in half. Then another. Pretty soon, we were begging and borrowing from anyone we could, but little by little we carved out our tunnel to freedom.

It took hours. We dug out one car, then another, and made a thin path to the main road. Soon, the guys and I were chanting, "Manifest destiny," as we reached an almost euphoric state, seeing the main road ahead. We completed our path to glory, stepped back, smiled, and collapsed in exhaustion. We had done it. We had beaten the Snow Monster of 2013. Nothing could stop us now.

Nothing, that is, except the giant plow truck that was making its way down our street. We stood back in horror as the truck barreled down our road, and in an attempt to do us good, buried every car we had dug out under seven feet of snow. Our tunnel was gone, our cars were invisible, and our efforts were completely wasted. Those neighbors who hadn't participated in our little escapade slowly, quietly, backed their cars out of their driveways, onto the freshly plowed road, and drove over to see what had happened.

"It's a shame about your cars," they said, with a smile.

"Thanks," we replied.

Nothing ignites the human spirit like a challenge. We are hardwired by God to push the boundaries, dream new dreams, and accomplish what was impossible for the generation before us. But just as we thrive in the face of a noble challenge, we also crumble in the face of wasted effort. When you give your very best and still fall painfully short, the subtle enemy that is despair begins to speak. And he can be hard to ignore.

Maybe you've heard the ancient Greek legend of Sisyphus. Sisyphus was a king who mocked the gods and was punished for his arrogance. He would wake up every morning at the foot of a hill and find within himself an insatiable urge to push a great boulder to the top. Sisyphus would try to resist, but the urge would eventually get the best of him. He would sweat and toil and work all day, until the boulder was just below the crest of the hill. Then, the massive boulder would slip from his hands and roll back down to the bottom. He'd wake up the next morning at the foot of the same hill, with the same boulder and the same urge. This went on forever.

The legend of Sisyphus is an indictment on the human condition. Something within us longs to conquer and succeed, and yet much of life is met with toil. This is no mistake. It's part of the original curse of sin that suffocates the Earth. God speaks this way to Adam in the Garden after Adam's sin:

> The ground is cursed because of you. All your life, you will struggle to scratch a living from it. It will grow thorns and this-tles for you... By the sweat of your brow will you have food to eat until you return to the ground from which you were made. For you were made from dust, and to dust you will return. (Gen. 3:17–19 NLT)

The sin of humanity has produced this frustrating reality. Effort is wasted, toil is endless, and change is hard to come by. I'm sure you've felt this frustration in your own life. Maybe you've experienced it at work, when the job that you deserve goes to someone less qualified, or in your physical body, when the surgery you had didn't fix the problem. Maybe you've tried to save money for something special, but every time you get ahead, another thing breaks unexpectedly and you have to spend what you saved. Toil. Frustration.

The toil on the outside, however, is only a reflection of the toil on the inside. Inwardly, every one of us wrestles with sin. Maybe it's your temper that frequently gets the best of you. You want to be patient, but as soon as your wife or your son or your employee messes up, you see red. Or maybe it's that subtle addiction that you thought you would have conquered years ago—that need for a drink, that dependence on a pill, or that secret sexual compromise. No one knows, and you act like it doesn't exist. But you know. And God knows.

Have you ever felt like Sisyphus, pushing the same boulder up the same hill only to see it roll to the bottom again? Have you ever felt the ache of useless toil and been confronted with your desperate inability to change? I have. I've felt this way at times, battling thoughts of fear or lust or condemnation and not knowing why those thoughts wouldn't go away. What's wrong with me? I love Jesus, I believe in the gospel, yet this brokenness seems to linger. Where do I turn?

Often our response to this frustration is to remember God's moral law, "Be holy, for I am holy." (1 Peter 1:16) The command inspires us, but it doesn't empower us. In fact, sometimes knowing what is right creates a greater desire to do what is wrong. Sometimes the temptation doesn't even exist until we are told not to do it, and then it becomes appealing and alluring. What is broken inside of us? How do we break free from this bondage?

The apostle Paul laments this frustration in his letter to the Romans when he writes, "For I have the desire to do what is right, but not the ability to carry it out… Wretched man that I am! Who will deliver me from this body of death?" (Rom. 7:18, 24) Sisyphus tells us that no one will. You are trapped, condemned to toil for the rest of your days frustrated and fruitless.

But that is not the message of Jesus. Through the truth of the *covenant*, we discover that God speaks the language of promise. Through the truth of the *atonement*, we realize the revelation of his love. Through the truth of *justification*, we experience divine assurance. And through the truth of *adoption*, we establish authentic relationship with our Father. But it's through the truth of the *resurrection* that we receive power.

There All Along

Years ago, I read a biography of Winston Churchill. As a young man in the British Army, Churchill participated in one of Britain's last legitimate cavalry charges.[1] This means men on horses with swords, galloping toward the enemy. By the time he was prime minister of Britain, he was discussing plans to use the nuclear bomb. Think of this: from horses and swords to nuclear bombs, in one man's lifetime. That's a significant change.

Over the course of one generation, technology changed so quickly. But how? It required a scientific revolution. A few hundred years ago, humanity was living with horses and candles, and today we have airplanes and LED lights. From Benjamin Franklin to Albert Einstein, men and women discovered that there are forces on this Earth available for greater use. Electricity, fossil fuel—all these things existed in 1701, but no one knew how *to take what was available and connect it to what was needed.* In order to access the power available, people needed to embrace a new perspective. They needed to see something that was already there.

What is true in the natural is an even greater truth in the spirit. God himself *is* ultimate reality. He doesn't just define right and wrong; he defines what is and what isn't. If God says, "This is a fact," then no one has the right to argue with him, since he has a clearer view of things than we do.

Paul introduces the perspective of God when he writes:

So, my brothers and sisters, you also died to the law through the body of Christ, that you might belong to another, to him who was raised from the dead, in order that we might bear fruit for God. (Rom. 7:4 NIV)

Notice the tense. We *have* died? How could that be? The verses before this statement bring some clarity.

Do you not know, brothers and sisters … that the law has authority over someone only as long as that person lives? For example,
by law, a married woman is bound to her husband as long as he
is alive, but if her husband dies, she is released from the law that
binds her to him. (7:1–2 NIV)

There is something here that we must *know*, that's why Paul begins with
"Do you not know…" Your relationship to the curse of sin is like a marriage. You both said "I do," and you have been bound to sin ever since.
But if the husband or wife dies, the marriage ends and the connection
is broken. But since I'm not dead, and sin is not dead, how can I be free
from this bad marriage?

You can't—unless *you are* in fact dead.

We know that our old self was crucified with him in order that
the body of sin might be brought to nothing, so that we would
no longer be enslaved to sin. (6:6)

Your identification with Christ extends to his death and resurrection. In
other words, Jesus came to identify with humanity as our representative
and, just as Adam represented all of humanity when he sinned, and the
curse of sin was passed to all of Adam's children, so Christ represented all
of humanity in his righteousness.

This is why, through his death, he could justify all those who believe. His righteous record is mine, but his death is also mine! In other
words, according to the perspective of God, (who *is* ultimate reality),
when Christ died, I died with him! He was buried; I was buried. His life
ended; my life ended. According to God, my old life was crucified and
died with Jesus on the cross! This is how he sees it, and therefore this is
how I must see it.

When Jesus died, I died, meaning that the legal right of sin was severed in my life because death ended the marriage. This all *actually happened* from the invisible perspective of God, and it happened "that you might belong to another." In other words, you didn't stay single long. Your death to sin through the body of Jesus betrothed you to your true love.

> Therefore, a man shall leave his father and mother and hold fast to his wife, and the two shall become one flesh. This mystery is profound, and I am saying that it refers to Christ and the church. (Eph. 5:31–32)

The moment you put your faith in Jesus and his Spirit came into your heart, your old life ended, and you were made one in marriage with Christ! This, of course, sounds strange to our natural minds. How can we be married to God? What we need to grasp is that marriage is an earthly shadow of an eternal spiritual truth. Just as a husband and wife physically become one through intimacy, so God has become one with his people. In a marriage, everything that belongs to one spouse now belongs to both husband and wife. So everything that belongs to Christ now belongs to you! If you're one with Christ, his death is yours, his righteousness is yours, his relationship to the Father is yours—and his resurrection is yours!

> For if we have been united with him in a death like his, we shall certainly be united with him in a resurrection like his. (Rom. 6:5)

> If the Spirit of the One who resurrected Jesus from the dead lives inside of you, then you can be sure that He who raised Him will cast the light of life into your mortal bodies through the life-giving power of the Spirit residing in you. (8:11 Voice translation)

Consider this! Read it again if you have to! Maybe you need to put this book down for a minute and dance around your room! God is saying that his resurrection power already resides *in* you! Just like fossil fuels and electricity, it's been there all along! For generations, people walked right past the solution they needed, until they connected the dots and accessed the resources available. Then, the impossible was accomplished!

Charles Spurgeon puts it like this:

All-sufficient grace dwells in you, believer! There is a living well springing up within you; use the bucket, then; keep on drawing; you will never exhaust it; there is a living source within.[2]

When Paul prayed for the church in Ephesus, he didn't pray that God would give them extra power from heaven. Instead, he prayed that the eyes of their hearts would be opened so that they could see the *immeasurable greatness of his power toward us who believe* (Eph. 1:18–19). He wanted them to see the power they already had. And where is it? *In your inner being* (2:16). God's power to break the cycle of slavery to sin already exists within you.

God has deposited his infinite reservoir of power into your inner being through Jesus so that you can overcome temptation from sin here and now. But how? How do we experience the power that God has made available? How do we finally get that boulder to the top of the hill? How do we break the cycle of habitual addiction or fear or compulsion in our lives?

Power Now

Scripture provides an answer for how we can experience the power of God over sin day by day. We'll devote the last chapter to the process, but the answer begins with a change in perspective.

So you also must consider yourselves dead to sin and alive to God in Christ Jesus. (Rom. 6:11)

Consider yourself. The Old English translations use the word *reckon*. The word literally means to *calculate or compute an equation*. Add everything up. Do the math, and come up with your answer. Add up Adam's sin, God's law, the shadows of the Old Testament, God's language of covenant, and his sacrifice of atonement. Add up Christ as your representative, justification through his perfect record, and the legal decree that *it is finished*. Add up the adoption given to us as sons, and the new relationship we have with the Father. Your death through the crucifixion of Jesus, and your resurrection through his new life. The calculation might seem like Latin at first, but learn his equation and come up with your answer. When you do, you will find that everything adds up perfectly.

The power of sin is broken. You are free *in Jesus's name*.

For this to become of any use in your life, God's perspective must become more real to you than your natural perspective. Meditate on it until the truth begins to dawn on your heart. See your old life on the cross with Jesus. See your new life risen from the dead and married to Christ.

I died with Jesus. Sin's authority over me has ended. I no longer need to live in slavery.

Consider yourself dead to sin and alive to God. Paul calls this "walking in newness of life." (6:4) It means that I am living empowered by the realities of a new age. God's perspective has become more real to me than my own natural perspective. Even when I see things differently, I align my point of view with his. He says I'm dead, buried, and risen. He says the legal rights of sin over my life have been canceled. He says I'm free, and he sees me more accurately than I see myself.

It was years ago when I first stumbled onto Romans 6 and was baffled by what it said. At that point, I was struggling with the same sins again and again, seeing little progress and feeling a lot like Sisyphus. I had tried everything I could think of to be free from the cycle of these sinful habits. I had begged God for the strength to change but saw little transformation.

I remember getting to the point of pure exhaustion and exclaiming out loud, "If God can't set a man free, then what is all of this? How can it be true if it doesn't have power? God, if you are who you say you are, show me how to change!"

Then I landed on Romans 6, and something started to shift in my inner being. A new hope began to dawn on my soul.

I am dead to sin and alive to God.

To embrace this perspective is an act of faith, and *faith connects the power you need to the power you already have.* Faith is the electrical conductor of God's power. When you rely on God, depend on God, and believe what he says, his power is released in your life to accomplish what would otherwise be impossible. *The power to change is discovered through a new perspective.* It's realized as you recognize what is already yours.

I read about a man in Nevada who died alone in his home. Walter Samaszko Jr. died at 69 years old from heart problems. At the time of his death, he had $200 in the bank. He had no friends, no will, and no known relatives. When the authorities came to clean out his home, they found in his garage a shoebox full of rare coins that turned out to be worth nearly $7 million.[3] Walter could have lived in a palace. He could have traveled the world. With that much money, he had endless options available to him, but instead he died alone in a small home outside the city.

Maybe he just didn't know the value of what he had in his garage. Maybe he never took the time to consider its worth. Maybe he never did the math and added everything up, and came to an accurate conclusion.

We will never know what stopped Walter Samaszko from using the wealth he had available to him, but the story should cause us to pause. What has God given me that I've left in the garage? What has Christ afforded me that I've kept buried in a shoebox?

For sin will have no dominion over you, since you are not under law but under grace. (6:14)

The law showed me what to do, but didn't empower me to do it. Grace teaches me a new language, and a new equation. Add it up and you will find that the answer is *life* itself.

DISCUSSION QUESTIONS

1. What stood out to you in this chapter? What did you learn? What did you find most helpful?

2. Scripture tells us that the Spirit who raised Jesus from the dead lives in us. That means God has given us an infinite reservoir of his power. This power is exercised when we overcome sin, extend love or forgiveness, or boldly share our faith. Talk about times in your spiritual journey when you have experienced the power of the Holy Spirit. What impact has his power had on your life?

3. The Scripture teaches that you are dead to sin and alive to God. You are free from the power of sin. Faith is needed to embrace this perspective. Spiritual disciplines can give faith room to grow. These disciplines include daily time with God and reading the Bible, prayer, accountability to other believers, active participation in a local church, sexual purity, and financial stewardship. Talk about the disciplines you embrace now that you know strengthen your spiritual life. What may be hindering you from fully embracing consistent spiritual disciplines? What practical steps will you take this week to grow your faith?

7

Sanctification

Work out your own salvation with fear and trembling, for it is God who works in you, both to will and to work for his good pleasure.

—Philippians 2:12–13

The date was Thursday, December 12, 1799. George Washington was in good health and good spirits. He spent the morning on horseback, supervising work at Mount Vernon. Then in the afternoon, the weather shifted. It started to snow, then hail, and then rain. Like many nights for the first American president, this one would be spent entertaining guests.

By the time he came in from work, the evening festivities were already beginning, and rather than hurry upstairs and change, Washington decided to stay in his wet clothing and begin welcoming his guests. He didn't want to be late.

Hours passed, and when Washington woke up the next morning, he realized that he had caught a cold. On December 14, just two days after his dinner party, 67-year-old George Washington, the Father of the United States of America, was dead.[1]

For generations, historians and medical experts have debated the details of Washington's death. There are dozens of theories and opinions, but one aspect is beyond question: his choice to stay in cold, wet clothing made him sick.

In the life of the believer, sin is like George Washington's wet clothes. It tries to come with you into the great banquet, and you may even entertain excuses for why it shouldn't be removed. But deep down at your core, you know that the wet clothing must go. To keep it on makes you sick, and you can't enjoy the banquet until you're wearing new clothes.

Salvation by grace through faith is one of the greatest mysteries uncovered through the gospel. We discover that God's love compelled him to come, take on flesh, stand in our place, and pay our debt. When a person repents and believes in Christ, God's Holy Spirit takes up residence in his heart. Scripture describes it this way:

> Therefore, if anyone is in Christ, he is a new creation. The old has passed away; behold the new has come. (2 Cor. 5:17)

There now resides within the believer a new spirit, and this spirit is united with God's Spirit in the hidden place of the heart. Because your spirit is born of God, you now have the DNA of God written on the inside. You are, at your core, a new creation. And with this new life come new desires. The apostle John describes this inner change when he writes:

> No one born of God makes a practice of sinning, for God's seed abides in him; and he cannot keep on sinning, because he has been born of God. (1 John 3:9)

God's seed abides in you, and you cannot painlessly continue to practice the pattern of sin like you used to. But not every old desire evaporates overnight. Some do, and we should thank God for that. Sometimes the moment of encounter with God changes us so profoundly that we never touch an old sin again. But other times, the process is not so instant. Some sins don't leave without a fight.

Scripture outlines three enemies in your pursuit of godliness. The first is your *spiritual* enemy. Demonic forces seek to pull you away from God. The second is your *systemic* enemy. The systems and culture of the world will try to draw your devotion away from God. The third is your *internal* enemy. You have the Spirit of Jesus in the house of Adam. In other words, the impulses of your flesh will war against the Spirit of Christ within you.

Sin's legal right to you was canceled through the resurrection of Jesus. When he died, you died with him, and when he rose again, you were given access to new life. The power of sin is broken, but the daily experience of sin lingers. How does the follower of Jesus conquer sin and become more like Christ?

The Scripture calls this process *sanctification*. Notice that John describes the work of God in our hearts like a seed. *God's seed abides in him.* A seed doesn't become a great tree in a day, or a month, or a year. It's a process that is occurring every moment, and though it often may look like nothing is happening, when you step back and look over the course of time, the results are amazing.

Sanctification simply means to be set apart for holy purposes. In the Old Testament, the priests would set apart certain silverware or utensils for use in the temple. These items were *sanctified*. Theologian Wayne Grudem defines sanctification as "a progressive work of God and man that makes us more and more free from sin and like Christ in our actual lives."[2] If you are a Christian, then you are already on the journey of sanctification.

Working Hard or Hardly Working

There are two errors that every Christian will have to confront in sanctification. The first error is that holiness is not essential to the Christian life. It's possible to hear about the goodness of God and think, *God has*

made atonement for me, justified me, and adopted me. I have no obligation to
live holy, since he has already forgiven me.

It is true that God has already forgiven you, and his forgiveness is not
based on your merits or good works. Your acceptance is entirely based
on Christ's good works. But it's also true that he accomplished this work
so that he could place his Spirit *within* you. Since his Spirit is the Holy
Spirit, it's impossible to have his Spirit and not long for holiness. In other
words, if I profess faith in Jesus, but don't long to be holy, then my faith
isn't saving faith. I may accept Jesus intellectually, but God's seed does
not abide in me. If it did, I would thirst for holiness.

The second error, however, is to think that Jesus died for my sins,
and now I must earn my place with him through a life of good works. But
this makes my sanctification (my holy works) the cause of my salvation,
and God says that grace alone is the cause of my salvation (Eph. 2:8).
Sanctification is not the cause of salvation, it's the result of salvation. It
acts as a sign or evidence that God's Spirit really does live inside you.

> For by a single offering, he has perfected for all time those who
> are being sanctified. (Heb. 10:14)

Did you catch that? God has already perfected you in Jesus. And at the
same time, you are in the middle of the perfection process! In other
words, sanctification (the ongoing process of becoming more like Jesus)
flows from justification (the legal decree that you are forgiven and Christ's
righteousness belongs to you). This is critical, because trying really hard
to become more and more holy isn't the most effective way to actually
grow in holiness.

Think back to the story *The Prince and the Pauper*: two boys who
look identical, but one is the future king, and the other is a kid from the
slums. Physically, they were the same, but one of them thought like a
king, and it changed the way he perceived everything.

God's method for Christians to become holy isn't to try harder, it's to think differently. The most effective way to grow in holiness is to deeply internalize what Christ has done for you. Keller puts it this way:

> Sanctification is not by "works" but by a continuous reorienting ourselves to our justification... When we feed on, remember, and live in accordance with our justification, it mortifies our idols and fills us with an inner joy and desire to please and resemble our Lord through obedience. But the feeding on, remembering, and living in accordance—takes all our effort.[3]

Kevin DeYoung reiterates this sentiment when he writes, "The secret of the gospel is that we actually do more when we hear less about all we need to do for God and hear more about all that God has already done for us."[4]

The more you internalize what God has done for you, the more you become what God says you are: a child of God, filled with his Spirit and set apart for his glory.

Becoming Who You Are

The good news of what Jesus has done fundamentally changes the motivations of the heart. When a follower of Jesus hasn't deeply internalized the gospel, the natural inclination is to obey God out of fear of judgment. *You better be good, or God will take away your job, or ruin your plans, or strike your spouse with an illness.* Most of us wouldn't admit to thinking that way, but that line of thought often seeps into our motives for holiness. The gospel suffocates fear once and for all.

> There is no fear in love. But perfect love drives out fear, because fear has to do with punishment. The one who fears is not made perfect in love. (1 John 4:18 NIV)

As the perfect love of God works its way into your heart through the gospel, fear slowly dissolves and a new motive rises to the top. This new motive is *delight*.

> I delight in your decrees; I will not neglect your word.
> (Psalm 119:16 NIV)

A simple truth begins to dawn on the soul: *God is for me! He has proven his intentions through the cross. He is more committed to my good than I am! He's working everything for my good, therefore, any command he gives me is ultimately to make me happier!*

The limits and commands of God are changed in your mind from rules that hinder your fun to boundaries that maximize your joy! They aren't burdensome decrees anymore. They are *life* and *peace*! This is the secret to overcoming the war of sin in your heart.

> Do not conform to the pattern of this world, but be transformed
> by the renewing of your mind. (Rom. 12:2 NIV)

You and I are transformed when we think differently about God and life and sin. This new perspective is the foundation of what Paul meant when he told us to "work out [our] salvation." It's progressive and it grows over the course of our time on Earth, all the way until the moment we see Jesus face to face.

But what are we supposed to do? First, we play a *passive* role in our growth in holiness. Our passive role is to surrender. We must surrender every part of our lives into the hands of God (12:1). Don't cling to anything. Surrender your future, your past, your present, your plans, your resources, your desires—everything. As we trust God with everything, his Spirit takes the leadership role in our lives, and the result is tremendous growth. It is God who causes the growth in our hearts and matures us as we surrender. His invisible work within us changes the believer day by day to become more like Christ.

But we also take an *active* role in sanctification. This means that we do everything in our natural abilities to fight sin and run from temptation. If you're an alcoholic, don't hang out at the bar. If you have a history of sexual addiction, don't surf the internet alone at two o'clock in the morning. Frequently in the New Testament, Christians are instructed to "make every effort." (See Luke 13:24, Rom. 14:19, and Eph. 4:3 as examples.) This means that we embrace accountability, study the Bible, pray often, worship God, gather with other Christians frequently, and share about Christ with others. Pursue holiness with all your heart, and do it because you *delight* in the love of God. But you also need to do it with the revelation that you *can't* do it.

Fear and Trembling

Right after Paul tells the church to *"work out your salvation,"* he tells them to do it "with fear and trembling." Fear and trembling? I thought we weren't supposed to be afraid? I thought perfect love casts out all fear?

Just like there is more than one kind of love (like love for pizza versus love for your wife), there is also more than one kind of fear. Paul is not referring to a fear of wrath and judgment from God. This fear, as New Testament scholar Gordon Fee puts it, "reflects human vulnerability."[5] This is a deep internal awareness that you are unable to perform at the level God requires. No matter how hard you try, no matter how diligent you are, you can't do it. You can fight and strive and struggle and plead, but there is a darkness in you that you cannot conquer. To be ignorant of that darkness is to be enslaved by it. To pretend like that darkness doesn't exist is to be deceived by it. The only person who is truly free is the one who stares at the darkness abiding in their own soul and honestly, humbly presents it to Jesus. Then, true freedom can be realized.

We are flawed and broken vessels, but God's light shines through our cracks and imperfections. We have the Spirit of Jesus in the house of Adam, and this reality humbles us. Yet, with the realization of our own inability to fix ourselves, we discover that God works his power through our weakness.

> Each time, he said, "My grace is all you need. My power works best in weakness." So now I am glad to boast about my weaknesses, so that the power of Christ can work through me. That's why I take pleasure in my weakness... For when I am weak, then I am strong. (2 Cor. 12:9–10 NLT)

I take pleasure in my weakness? What's pleasurable about being weak?

> Blessed are the poor in spirit, for theirs is the kingdom of heaven. (Matt. 5:3)

We can take pleasure in our weaknesses because God blesses those who realize their absolute need for him. When we embrace our own spiritual poverty, God doesn't just welcome us. He gives us the kingdom! The revelation of my weakness is the secret to my victory!

So the process of sanctification entails reorienting ourselves to our justification, embracing the passive role of surrender and the active role of fighting sin, while at the same time deeply acknowledging that we are dark and broken and cannot do it! This may feel a bit overwhelming, and that's why God included verse 13.

> For it is God who works in you, both to will and to work for his good pleasure. (Phil. 2:13)

You are not the primary agent in your sanctification, God is. You cooperate with God, but he is the force behind your victory.

John Ortberg compares sanctification to sailing when he says, "When I'm sailing... I have a definite role to play. I hoist the sails. I steer the rudder... but I am utterly dependent on the wind. If the wind doesn't blow, I'm dead in the water. When the wind blows, on the other hand, amazing things can happen."[6]

God is the wind, and I am the sailboat. He promises to work in me to transform my desires and empower my effort. Consider for a moment the implications of this promise. New Testament scholar Gordon Fee writes on verse 13:

> God is on the side of his people... he not only has their concern at heart, but actively works in their behalf for the sake of his own good pleasure... Thus, the one supplying the power for your obedience is none other than the living God.[7]

Hold on a minute. Take a deep breath. God works in you, to *will* and *work* his good pleasure? The one who created the universe, who holds the stars in their place, who designed the cosmos and died on the cross—the infinite, omniscient Creator God—works *in* you to make you holy?

God will always supply the power you need for an act of obedience.

If you will reorient your thinking around the gospel, pursue holiness with your whole heart, and present your brokenness to Jesus, he will empower you day by day to conquer the sin in your soul. Think of it: freedom from anxiety, victory over lust, dominion over insecurity. It doesn't necessarily mean that the problem goes away. Sometimes it lingers. Sometimes it shows up every morning. But it does mean that God will give you the grace you need for the obedience of the moment. In this way, we stay dependent and humble and free. Let the words of Charles Spurgeon encourage your soul.

He that gave you the will does not leave you there; He works in you the divine power to do. The power to achieve the victory, the power to smite down the loftiest plume of pride shall come from Him. God is equal to all emergencies, therefore fear not; though your inner life shall be subject to ten thousand dangers, He will give you power to do the right, the just, the lovely and the true; for He works gloriously in you.[8]

Taking the Step

Remember Indiana Jones in his pursuit of the Holy Grail? He reaches a chasm that is too far to jump across. At first, moving forward seems hopeless. He's come so far and has gotten so close, and yet the great chasm stands between him and his treasure. Then he remembers the legend of the invisible bridge. This test was called The Leap of Faith. He has to step out on the bridge while it remains invisible to him. Once he takes the step, he discovers that there is in fact a path that leads across. At first he hesitates, then finally takes the plunge, and his feet find the invisible bridge.

Maybe conquering a certain sin feels to you like that chasm. You've tried a thousand times and you're worse today than you were before. The addiction still defeats you. The fear still controls you. The anger still dominates you. You've read the last few chapters, but you don't *feel* the power of God to overcome. Instead you feel tempted and weak and vulnerable.

The Old Testament tells the story of Joshua as he led the people of Israel into the Promised Land. They had spent 40 years in the desert, Moses had died, and the day had come for them to receive the promise. The only thing between them and their promise was a raging river. God instructed the priests to walk into the river.

Now the Jordan is at flood stage all during harvest. Yet as soon as the priests who carried the ark reached the Jordan and their feet touched the water's edge, the water from upstream stopped flowing...while the water flowing down...was completely cut off. So the people crossed. (Josh. 3:15–16 NIV)

Imagine what those priests were thinking with the Ark of the Covenant on their shoulders, as they stepped into a raging river. The current was strong enough to rip them downstream, and there they stood on the banks. Couldn't they command the river to part *before* they stepped in? Why did they need to get in the river before God worked the miracle? Because this story contains a powerful truth about your promised land.

The power of the Spirit is released when you take the first step.

Not before, not after. The moment you take the first step, God meets you with a rushing overflow of his power. In doing this, he teaches you the habit of dependence on him, while empowering you to accomplish what was impossible without him.

Over the years I've watched this principle prove true in my own life and in the lives of countless others. Recently, I met with a friend who confessed his battle with sexual addiction. He told me his story and asked if he could share his struggles with me when he failed. I told him he could, but that confession alone wouldn't break the cycle. Instead, I asked him to pick up the phone and call me in his next moment of temptation, before any sin had transpired. Any hour, anytime.

By reaching out for prayer before sin had taken hold, he was taking the first step onto the invisible bridge. Once he does that, the power of God is released, the temptation is exposed in his heart as a lie, and its grip on his soul dissipates.

God's power is released when *you take* the first step. So God works in you, giving you the desire to be holy and the power to live holy, and he does it all for a specific purpose: *for his good pleasure* (Phil. 2:13). For many of us, that phrase doesn't sit quite right. His good pleasure?

I thought he worked in me for my good pleasure? Gordon Fee shines some light on this tension.

> All that God does he does for his pleasure; but since God is wholly good, his doing what pleases him is not capricious but what is wholly good for those he loves. God's pleasure is pure love, so what he does "for the sake of his good pleasure" is by that very fact also on behalf of those he loves. After all, it delights God to delight his people.[9]

It delights God to delight his people. That may be the most encouraging news we've uncovered so far! God's glory and my happiness run on parallel tracks. When God acts for his good pleasure, his good pleasure is my good! Once and for all, I can rest. Once and for all, I can know beyond a doubt that no matter what happens in life, God is *for* me. And that truth brings a harvest of peace.

The Discipline of Forgetting

The apostle Paul gives us an incredible piece of advice on our journey of sanctification.

> Not that I have already obtained all this, or have already arrived at my goal, but I press on to take hold of that for which Christ Jesus took hold of me. Brothers and sisters, I do not consider myself yet to have taken hold of it. But one thing I do: forgetting what is behind and straining toward what is ahead, I press on toward the goal. (Phil. 3:12–14 NIV)

Jesus took hold of him, called him out of darkness, and into his marvelous light. It's through the covenant that God teaches us his language of promise. Through his atonement, God teaches us that he loves us with an undying love. Through our justification, God teaches us to rest in perfect assurance. Through our adoption, God teaches us to interact with him as our Father. Through the power of his resurrection, God teaches us to access the power within. And through sanctification, God changes us day by day into his likeness. In light of all of this, Paul tells us to forget.

Forget? Forget what?

Forget who you thought you were apart from God. Forget who you thought God was apart from the gospel. Forget every broken distortion that your mind has entertained about his character. Forget the pattern of sin that has gotten the best of you in the past. Forget the deep affections that you developed for other things. For approval, for comfort, for attention, or for self-glory.

C. S. Lewis famously said, "Humility is not thinking less of yourself, it's thinking of yourself less," and this is only possible when you are captivated by the astonishing work of Jesus through the gospel. Forget your past failures and forget your past success. Don't build your life on comparisons with your neighbor or the accomplishments of your career. His accomplishments for you build the foundation of true identity. His victory for you is the secret of a deeply satisfied soul. His love for you cures—once and for all—the disease of a broken, divided heart.

Remember again the words of Spurgeon:

The gospel is the sum of wisdom; an epitome of knowledge; a treasure-house of truth; and a revelation of mysterious secrets... Our meditation upon it enlarges the mind and, as it opens to our souls in successive flashes of glory, we stand astonished at the profound wisdom manifest in it. Ah, dear friends! If ye seek wisdom, ye shall see it displayed in all its greatness... Here is essential wisdom; enthroned, crowned, glorified.

Let these truths enlarge your mind and become for you a treasure-house. Soak in them every day until they deeply rewire your view of reality. I believe that right now God is retraining a generation of Christ-followers, teaching us how to think. The days of earning God's favor are over. The days of accepting sinful patterns and acting like there is no freedom—those days are over too. God wants you to know and believe the love he has for you. He wants you to live rooted and grounded in love. He wants you to wager your entire life on his grace. When you do, you reflect his glory.

What's your next step as you follow Jesus? None of us can take this journey alone, and these truths only become real in the context of community. Talk about them, wrestle through them with others. Invest deeply in relationships in God's family, the church. Memorize the promises outlined in this book. Tell others the news that God is *for* them and that he loves them with an everlasting love. As you do these things, God works in you. Through the process, you discover his heart, and as you do, you discover yourself. Don't waste another minute.

Believe.

And watch what God can do.

DISCUSSION QUESTIONS

1. Begin this week's discussion with an overview of the chapter. What was most helpful to you? What seemed confusing? How did this chapter connect to the rest of what we have covered in this book?

2. Christians face two errors in regard to sanctification. First, we can believe that holiness is not essential to Christian living. Second, we think our holy works will make us acceptable. Which falsehood do you tend to lean toward? Why do you think that is?

3. You learned in this chapter that sanctification (the ongoing process of becoming more like Jesus) flows from justification (the

legal decree that you are forgiven and Christ's righteousness belongs to you). This means that God's power is released not when you try harder but when you think differently. In light of this, what needs to change in your thinking?

4. In this chapter, you learned that there is a darkness in you that you cannot conquer. To be ignorant of that darkness is to be enslaved by it. To pretend like that darkness doesn't exist is to be deceived by it. The only person who is truly free is the one who stares at the darkness abiding in their own soul and honestly, humbly presents it to Jesus. What has this process looked like for you? How have you humbly confronted the darkness in your heart? How have you avoided it? What's your next step into the light?

5. The Scripture teaches that God will always supply the power you need for an act of obedience. What act of obedience is God calling you to right now? What is your next big step in obedience to God?

Notes

All Scripture quotations, unless otherwise indicated, are taken from the Holy Bible, English Standard Version.

Chapter 1: The Beauty

1. Wurmbrand, Richard. *Tortured for Christ*. Voice of the Martyr, 1969.
2. Spurgeon, Charles H. "Christ Crucified" in *Spurgeon's Sermons, Vol. 1* (Grand Rapids: Baker, 1996), p. 108–109.
3. Buechner, Frederick. *Telling the Truth: The Gospel as Tragedy, Comedy and Fairy Tale*. HarperOne, 1977, p. 96–97.

Chapter 2: Covenant

1. Tozer, A. W. *The Knowledge of the Holy: the Attributes of God: Their Meaning in the Christian Life*. HarperOne, 1992.
2. "Why Learn Latin?" *The Pegasus Project*, www.pegasusafterschool.org/whylearnlatin/.
3. Lockyer, Herbert. *All the Promises of the Bible*. Zondervan, 1962, p. 10.
4. Augustine, et al. *The Works of Aurelius Augustine A New Translation*. T. & T. Clark, 1872, p. 98.

Chapter 3: Atonement

1. Eldredge, John. *Wild at Heart*. Thomas Nelson Publishers, 2001, p. 188.

2. Keller, Timothy. *Look Inside: Center Church.* The Good Book Company, 2016, p. 31.

Chapter 4: Justification

1. Twain, Mark. *The Prince and the Pauper.* Longman, 1999.
2. Hooker, Richard and Izaak Walton. *The Work of Mr. Richard Hooker: In Eight Books of the Laws of Ecclesiastical Polity: with Several Other Treatises, and a General Index. Also, a Life of the Author.* W. Clarke, 1821, p. 341.
3. Packer, J. I. *Knowing God.* InterVarsity Press, 1973, p. 273.
4. Piper, John. *Fifty Reasons Why Jesus Came to Die.* Desiring God Foundation, 2008, p. 40–41.
5. Spurgeon, Charles. "The Weaned Child." Metropolitan Tabernacle, Newington.

Chapter 5: Adoption

1. Dean, Paul. "Who Was Steven? The Little Boy Who Had Been Kidnapped Never Found Himself." *Los Angeles Times,* September 22, 1989.
2. Feuerstein, Nathan. "I Can Feel It." *Therapy Session,* Capitol Christian Music Group, 2016, Track 8.
3. Keller, Timothy J. *Children of God.* Redeemer Presbyterian Church 2003, p. 231.
4. Henry, Matthew. *Matthew Henry's Commentary on the Whole Bible.* Hendrickson Publishers, 2009.
5. Ryan, Chris. "What Are the Odds of a High School Football Player Reaching the NFL?" *NJ.com,* Advance Local Media LLC, September 8, 2015, highschoolsports.nj.com/news/article/-1769497769554898414/what-are-the-odds-of-a-high-school-football-player-reaching-the-nfl/.
6. Packer, p. 202.

7. Fallon, Jimmy and Miguel Ordóñez. *Your Baby's First Word Will Be Dada.* Hodder Children's Books, 2017.

8. Ferguson, Sinclair B. *Children of the Living God.* The Banner of Truth Trust, 2011.

9. Keller, Timothy. *Prayer: Experiencing Awe and Intimacy with God.* Penguin Books, 2016, p. 172–173.

10. Miles, Charles Austin. "In the Garden." Public Domain, 1912.

11. Jakes, T. D. *Life Overflowing: The Spiritual Walk of the Believer.* Bethany House Publishers, 2003, p. 41.

Chapter 6: Resurrection

1. Niderost, Eric. "Battle of Omdurman: The Last British Cavalry Charge." *Warfare History Network,* October 31, 2016, warfarehistorynetwork.com/daily/military-history/battle-of-omdurman-the-last-british-cavalry-charge/.

2. Spurgeon, Charles. "Working Out What Is Worked In." 12 July, 1868, Metropolitan Tabernacle, Newington.

3. Murphy, Doyle. "Nevada Hoarder's Coins Sell for $3.2 Million at Auction." *New York Daily News,* August 7, 2013.

Chapter 7: Sanctification

1. "The Death of George Washington." *George Washington's Mount Vernon,* www.mountvernon.org/library/digitalhistory/digital-encyclopedia/article/the-death-of-george-washington/.

2. Grudem, Wayne. *Bible Doctrine: Essential Teachings of the Christian Faith.* InterVarsity Press, 2010.

3. "Monergism Interview with Dr. Tim Keller." *Monergismcom Blog,* www.monergism.com/thethreshold/articles/onsite/kellerinterview.html.

4. DeYoung, Kevin. "On Mission, Changing the World, and Not Being Able to Do It All." *The Gospel Coalition,* August 25,

2009, www.thegospelcoalition.org/blogs/kevin-deyoung/
on-mission-changing-world-and-not-being/.

5. Fee, Gordon D. *Paul's Letter to the Philippians*. Eerdmans, 1995, p. 236.

6. Duvall, J. Scott. *The Rescue: Salvation, the Holy Spirit, the Church*. Kregel Publications, 2009, p. 26.

7. Fee, p. 238.

8. Spurgeon, Charles. "Working Out What Is Worked In." 12 July, 1868, Metropolitan Tabernacle, Newington.

9. Fee, p. 240.